Broken Columns
Two Roman Epic Fragments

The Achilleid
of Publius Papinius Statius
AND
The Rape of Proserpine
of Claudius Claudianus

Broken Columns

Two Roman Epic Fragments

The Achilleid
of Publius Papinius Statius

AND

The Rape of Proserpine
of Claudius Claudianus

Translated by
DAVID R. SLAVITT
Afterword by David Konstan

PENN

University of Pennsylvania Press

Philadelphia

10 9 8 7 6 5 4 3 2 1

Published by
University of Pennsylvania Press
Philadelphia, Pennsylvania 19104-4011

Library of Congress Cataloging-in-Publication Data

Broken columns : two Roman epic fragments / translated by David R.
Slavitt ; afterword by David Konstan.
p.   cm.
Includes bibliographical references (p.   ).
Contents: The achilleid of Publius Papinius Statius—The rape of
Proserpine of Claudius Claudianus.
ISBN 0-8122-3424-3 (cloth)
1. Epic poetry, Latin—Translations into English. 2. Achilles
(Greek mythology)—Poetry. 3. Proserpina (Roman deity)—Poetry.
4. Mythology, Classical—Poetry. 5. Trojan War—Poetry.
I. Slavitt, David R., 1935–   . II. Statius, P. Papinius (Publius
Papinius). Achilleis. English. III. Claudianus, Claudius. De
raptu Proserpinae. English.
PA6164.B76   1997
873'.0109—dc21   97-34392
                                                              CIP

For Katharine and Tuck

Contents

.

Preface

PUBLIUS PAPINIUS STATIUS WAS BORN IN NAPLES between 45 and 60 A.D. in the reign of Domitian, which makes him what modern scholars call a Silver Age poet. His father, a schoolmaster, rhetorician, and poet, won prizes for his work at the Augustulia in Naples. Young Publius then grew up in a literary atmosphere, enriched more by the study of Virgil than by his vocation: he lived the hand-to-mouth existence of many poets, earning money from time to time from prizes or by giving readings, or getting help from some friendly amateurs of the arts—the wealthy Claudius Etruscus, the praetor Vitorius Marcellus, C. Vibius Maximus, prefect of Egypt, and Domitian's secretary Flavius Abascantus, among others—but apparently he never attached himself to any particular *patronus*. Still, he didn't do too badly, getting himself a villa and a grant of a special water supply from Domitian. He was a contemporary of Martial, but neither poet mentions the other—from which some scholars infer a certain coolness between them. He died probably in the winter of 95–96, but certainly before Domitian's death in September of 96.

He was known in the Middle Ages as a writer of epics—the *Thebaid* in twelve books, and the unfinished *Achilleid* in two. Dante, Alcuin of York, Boccaccio, and Chaucer all refer to him but mention only these works.

In 1417 Poggio discovered the *Silvae*, five books of occasional poems mostly in hexameters, and it was largely because of these that Statius' reputation grew during the Renaissance. The *Thebaid*, I think, is rather heavy going (although compared to Silius Italicus' even longer *Punica* it is a rip-snorting page turner). Still, Pope admired it and translated one book, and Goethe, too, found much to praise in Statius' epic work. The *Achilleid*, however, is another matter. An odd, even weird poem, it is very difficult not to like. First of all, it is only a fragment, but that seems to make it all the more attractive. The still-standing corner of a portico, requiring us as it does to imagine the complete temple, invites our collaboration, so that each observer's restoration can be informed by his or her own preferences. The original plan of the work, obviously, was to fill in the missing parts of the life of Achilles, but what Statius actually gives us first is a mannerist representation of the Thessalian hero in drag, hiding among the women on Scyros; then, in the second, unfinished book, we get Achilles' prep-school days. There is a vertiginous brashness here that I find irresistible.

Statius is not much read these days and should be better known and more widely enjoyed. What prompted me to undertake this rather breezy rendering was my conviction that he is a lively, vivid, and often very appealing poet, and my hope that particular fondness for his fragment might enable me to make some reasonable case for him. I have had help, of course. I have relied on O. A. W. Dilke's scrupulous Cambridge University Press edition, reprinted by the Arno Press, and have also consulted the H. H. Mozley translation in the Loeb Classical Library—in the Van Pelt Library of the University of Pennsylvania. (In Copy 3, some anonymous but very punctilious scholar has written, in tiny characters and in pencil, a number of valuable corrections and suggestions, several of which I have agreed with and adopted.)

The 1100 lines or so of the *Achilleid* make a rather slender volume, however. I also include, then, Claudian's *De Raptu Proserpinae*, a later epic fragment to which a reader can also supply as much or as little imaginative embellishment as seems appropriate. My own sense of the piece is that it is at the same time a defiant and a dejected work. The defiance I see in the choice of subject, the story of Ceres and Proserpine, which was what the Eleusinian mystery cult celebrated. The Christians were in power, Rome's old religion was outlawed, and Claudian was presenting, in a literary way, what was virtually forbidden material—almost like a public school teacher in contemporary America trying to smuggle a Bible into the classroom not as a religious book but only to demonstrate something of the fine qualities of Jacobean prose. Claudian seems to me an exile like Ovid, except that Ovid was sent off to Tomis where he could dream of the Rome from which he had been relegated, while Claudian, in Italy, had to watch as all around him the western Empire turned into a barbarian outpost, and undertook dream voyages that were temporal rather than spatial.

Claudius Claudianus has been called the last of the Roman poets, and Gibbon's faint praise of him is that he had "the rare talent of raising the meanest and adorning the most barren topics." Born in Alexandria in the later fourth century, he went to Italy and spent most of his literary energies writing panegyrics, particularly of Stilicho and of the emperors, and invectives against his enemies (or those of his patrons).

Whether his attempts at *The Rape of Proserpine* were prompted by piety or sheer orneriness is impossible to say. Hella Haasse, the contemporary Dutch writer, has a notion that Claudian may have been Jewish, and her novel about his life, *Threshold of Fire*, makes a series of unprovable, rather romantic, but nonetheless coherent suggestions about Claudian's life. Jack Schwartz of *Newsday* asked me to review this book when it appeared in Anita Miller and Nini Blinstrub's translation into English, and this assignment was what led me to Claudian's poem. The coincident publication in the Oxford Classical Monographs series of Claire Gruzelier's admirable edition and translation of, and commentary on, the poem seemed like a further prompting it would have been absurd to ignore.

The poem is a series of set pieces that have the stately charm of opera seria or, say, of those paintings in panels like Giotto's splendid work on the walls of the Scrovegni Chapel in Padua. Claudian's object is never breezy narrative, but a shrewd, collaborative, and even conspiratorial playing with the reader's expectations. We all know the story, and he knows that we're wondering how he will acquit himself at the next required figure, and the next. He does, very often, quite well, and he can be persuasive and even abruptly moving. His bit with the spider in Book III is, I think, one of the great moments of all Latin poetry. The tendency of classical studies to concentrate more and more on fewer and fewer texts has not been kind to Claudian. Attention, as Willy Loman says, should be paid.

The two poems together make an unlikely perfecta, and yet they do, in a way, go together after all. My old friend the young classicist Stephen Wheeler suggested a title that would have been appropriate for both pieces, and I was tempted to call the book *What's a Mother to Do?* But cooler heads prevailed. I thank Stephen, but I thank Eric Halpern at the University of Pennsylvania Press, too.

THE ACHILLEID

PUBLIUS PAPINIUS STATIUS

Book I

Of the great-spirited hero of Aeacus' line, of him
even the Thunderer feared to beget, lest, as Proteus
warned, the son might exceed the father, inheriting heaven,
goddess, tell—of that famous Achilles whose deeds immortal
Homer sang. But there is yet more of the story. Allow
me the honor; indulge my impossible aspirations;
let me fill in those gaps, commence at the very beginning
with Achilles hiding on Scyros, and spin out the rest of the tale
beyond his dragging of Hector's body around the walls
of doomed Troy to the bitter end of the war and of him.   10
Apollo, if you approved my earlier efforts, grant me
new inspiration, and weave those magical charms in my hair
as I essay again the holy task you invite
mortals to undertake. The story of Thebes I have told,
from Amphion's building the walls that leapt into place at his music
and the fountain of Dirce bubbling up on the plain where she died.
    And you, Domitian, who wear the double laurel of warrior-
poet, whom Greece and Rome regard with wonder and awe,
continue to show me your favor as I drudge away in the dust.
This recollection of splendor is dedicated to you,   20
from whom I extrapolate to Achilles' honor and strength.

    The shepherd from Troy had put to sea from Sparta's rocky
shore, having done there mischief, fulfilling his mother's dreadful
dream of the burning torch. Its tinder he carried now
back to the Hellespont, where Thetis, beneath the waves,

felt in the slosh of his oars' ominous eddies fear.
She and her sisters, startled, started forth from the frothy
waves to the airier heights of heaven. She drew a breath
and declared, "There is danger to me and mine. Of that baleful fleet
30   Bellona is navigator. What Proteus warned of once
is now coming true as a new daughter-in-law approaches
Priam's shore. I can see the keels of a thousand ships
churning their wakes across the Ionian Sea and Aegean:
the Greeks conspire, allied with the sons of Atreus' house,
and soon will come for my son, Achilles, and ask him to join
and fight with them. And to do so will be his own wild wish.
Was it for this that I sent him away to Chiron's cave,
to safe obscurity there? And what did he learn but to carry
deadly weapons and rough-house, as the centaurs did with the
        Lapiths,
40   turning social occasions to blood-baths? A mother's fears
clouded my judgment. I should have sunk those Trojan ships
on the westward leg of their voyage, while the kidnapper's deed
        was yet
a mere intention. The other nymphs and I together
could have stirred up a mighty storm, but it's too late now.
The crime is committed, and yet, perhaps by a greater power
something may still be done. I shall go to Jupiter's brother
to entreat mighty Neptune with a mother's supplication
that he grant me one great storm to founder the Trojan fleet."
    And there he was, the mighty god, come fresh from a banquet
50   Oceanus had prepared. The glow of the nectar still
lit his face, and the realms he governed were likewise placid,
the winds gentled, the waves refracting a shimmer of moonlight.
There was music too, as the Tritons, his armor bearers, sang
the chanteys and glees for which, in such moments as these,
he had displayed some fondness. As dolphins play in the waves
in the seas below, they danced and gamboled around him, adoring,
saluting their mighty lord. Thetis made bold to address him:
"Sire, you rule the mighty and terrible ocean where men
with dark purposes cross from one coast to the next,

as Jason did, in their quest of plunder. They pollute   60
your water as they profane its blue purity. Now
another crime is in progress, a different and far worse
theft, for the mortal who judged the goddesses on Ida
has gone to claim his prize—and a whole mountain of sorrows
will fall upon Greek and Trojan alike. Is this the gift
with which Venus rewards a compliment? Intercede,
I beg of you. The *Argo* was different: among its crew
were demigods who could claim immunity and protection.
These ships carry mere mortals. Drown them, or let me
do something less drastic, driving them off course   70
and far from home. I fear for my son. In sorrow, I beg.
Grant what I ask, or the wide ocean I live in will shrink
to a slice of Ilium's rocky beach in the sight of a tomb."
  Her cheeks were streaked with tears and her breast was bare as she
      grabbed
at the halter of Neptune's team of deep blue horses. The mighty
god of ocean, moved, helped the nymph climb aboard
his chariot. Then, in gentle and friendly words, he said
what he was obliged to say: "The fates that rule us all
will not permit such a thing. You know this, Thetis. That fleet
you'd wish to stop in its course is riding a mighty current   80
heaven has set in motion. Europe and Asia will meet
in a madness of death and fire. Greek and Trojan blood
will turn Ilium's grassy plain to a ghastly bog.
What awaits your son is glory, measured in Phrygian gore
and tears of widows and orphans who follow the funeral trains
of a hero's harvest of corpses. Those walls Apollo and I
together raised shall fall, razed by the righteous Argives'
anger. Peleus' son shall shine like the child of Jove
you wanted and do his father proud. I promise you comfort
and vengeance too—a storm when the fighting is done. Those
      Greeks   90
at Caphereus shall pay with wrecked ships, and their cries
of desperation shall satisfy you for selfish Ulysses'
scheming." He spoke, and she was unable to answer back.

With eyes cast down, disappointed, she thought of yet another
to whom she might turn in her need, in far-off Thessaly. Thither
she hurried, with mighty strokes, swimming, all but flying,
to wade ashore with the waves' white foam on her alabaster
ankles. The very landscape seemed to smile—this place
was where she had wedded Peleus. The mouth of the sea-cave gaped
100   wide, like a happy puppy's, and Spercheus' river water
purled about her feet in delighted greeting. She did not
acknowledge this welcome or notice, preoccupied as she was
with the trouble that weighed on her mind. She climbed the hill to
      Chiron's
lair carved in the rock of Pelion's flank, the centaur's
home and his sanctuary, for all about were the figures
of gods. No weapons of war hung on the walls, no spears
and swords that have bathed in human blood, but quivers and hides
of beasts he had hunted long ago in the years of his prime.
Unlike his boisterous brothers, Chiron had turned his attention
110   to the quiet study of plants' and herbs' medicinal uses.
To divert himself from this toil, he sometimes played on the lyre
and sang for himself and his pupils of the deeds of old-time heroes.
      While his charges were off in the woods, he was at home, preparing
a banquet to celebrate their return. He was laying the fire
when he happened to look up and notice the Nereid coming.
Thetis? It is! And he hurries, canters, excited to see her.
He trots down the path to greet her, his hoofbeats a lively tattoo
of welcome the woodland echoes. He bows at the waist in a decorous
courtliness and gives her a hand up to the cave mouth.
120   She enters and looks about her, adjusting her eyes to the lowered
light of the place. Is she troubled? Or is it merely the gloom?
"Where is my boy?" she asks him. "Why is he nowhere in sight?
I worry about his safety, which is why I gave him to you
to keep an eye on. But I do not see him, and neither can you.
My sleep is troubled, my dreams are awful, and nature provides
dismal omens and portents I wish I could disbelieve:
bared swords menace my belly; my arms are bruised
and my breasts torn by the fangs of beasts. What I did before

I must do again, return to the depths of Tartarus, dip him
once more in the murky waters of Styx. Proteus told me   130
how to protect him. I followed all his instructions, and yet
I worry. I grieve in advance. I am helpless, desperate, and watch
bright stars plummet and fall from the black sky into the black
maw of the sea to sizzle. I pray and sacrifice,
but am no less uneasy. It's no good. Give back my boy."
He could see how she was distracted but had no way of divining
the strange plan she had thought of. He could not have imagined
    the dress,
the wig, and the rest of the outfit she thought now to rely on,
or he'd never have given him up—as Thetis no doubt understood.
    "Take him," the centaur replied. "You are his mother and know   140
what's best for the boy. Your prayers, I am sure, will weigh with
    the gods.
I have had trouble myself with the lad, whose comportment is often
alarming. I cannot foresee what the gods have in store for him. Once
he accepted my direction, correction, and even my anger,
but now he ignores me and roams wherever he likes. This mountain
cannot contain him. The whole range is too small. He goes
wherever he wants, a mischief-maker, marauder . . . a plague
on herdsmen and farmers who see his spirited pranks as crimes.
And it's hard to argue when other centaurs come to complain,
or, lately, more often than not, to deliver their angry threats.   150
I remember, back in the days of the *Argo*, Theseus came here
with Hercules . . . " But there he broke off, for the goddess had
    turned
her head in relief and amazement as her son Achilles appeared
then in the clearing, covered with dust and sweat and . . . huge!
He bore his weapons, quiver and bow and spear, but smiled
nevertheless, a radiant grin for his mother. He looked
like a god! His hair was a golden halo. His eyes were bright
as fire. Try to imagine Apollo come back from a hunt
in exuberant mood, and Achilles could at that moment have posed
for the all but idealized statue. He has come from a lioness' lair   160
at the bottom of Pholoë's cliff. He has killed the mother and holds,

as his trophy, her cubs he means to tame as pets. But, seeing
his mother, he drops them and catches her up in his arms. He lifts
Thetis into the air. She can hardly breathe, in the grip
of her son and her own emotion. A few steps behind him, Patroclus
appears from the trees, Achilles' friend and companion who follows
now and will follow him further to Troy's heights and beyond.

    He puts her down and darts off to the nearby stream to wash
his face and hair and chest. Think of Castor, the horseman, the god,
170   dipping his star in the river Eurotas and then re-emerging
to shine the brighter in heaven. Chiron is struck anew
by the young man's beauty. The mother's delight is all she can bear.
The centaur invites them to eat and drink, and after the meal he
performs with the lyre to pluck on its strings that loosen the cords
of our cares. Then, for the mother's sake, to enjoy her delight,
he gives the instrument into Achilles' hands for the youth
to sing of the deeds of the great. Hercules' labors, he chooses
as subject, and Juno's wrath to which he was so long in thrall;
Pollux's fight he recounts, and how with his lead-lined cestus
180   he fought the ruthless Amycus and vanquished the Bebryces' king;
Theseus' struggle against the Cretan monster, the dreadful
Minotaur, he describes. But then, to acknowledge the happier
mood of the moment, he changes the subject from fighting to love
and sings of his mother's courtship and marriage banquet the gods
came down from the skies to attend on Pelion's heights. Thetis
is all smiles at her son, their host, and the grand occasion.
The wine has begun to produce its effect in the guests, who yawn,
agreeably full and sleepy. The centaur stretches out
on his couch, where Achilles lies down beside him—his usual place
which he chooses, no doubt, from habit even though his mother is
190   there.

    Thetis, unable to sleep, walks out of the cave and down
the hill to where the wavelets break on the beach with a murmur
soothing to troubled souls. She paces up and down,
thinking of hiding places in which she might best conceal
her child. One notion gives way to another. She thinks first of Thrace,
which isn't too far away . . . But the people there have a passion

for making war. No good, then. Macedon, possibly? No,
a not-quite-civilized place, hardy but too rough-and-tumble.
Athens, perhaps? They are surely cultivated, and yet
their curious notions of honor can lead to uncivil results.   200
Sestos? Or Abydos? No, on the ground that their harbors invite
ships that pass every day. A rather more distant island
in the Cyclades, perhaps? She considers Myconos, Lemnos,
Seriphos, Delos, but . . . Ah, on Lycomedes' island, on Scyros,
they lead an idyllic existence, with bands of young ladies dancing
and weaving their garlands of flowers. It's the last place a recruiter
would think to find a gallant soldier these days—and Thetis
remembers the place from years before when the son of Uranus,
Aegaeon, was captive there, that valiant fighter whose hundred
arms she had seen for herself. It was calmer now, even sleepy,   210
and nicely out of the way. She thought like a nervous bird
about to lay her eggs, looking to find the right bough
on which she might hang her nest—inconspicuous, safe,
a refuge for both herself and her soon-to-be-born fledglings.
After endless erratic flitting from this place to that,
she alights on the branch that somehow feels right and her heart is
         soothed.
   But the turmoil begins again, for now she must figure out ways
and means to get there, how, without attracting notice,
to carry her son to that island. By herself? With Triton's help?
Or Iris' perhaps? But better, she calls to her swimming dolphins   220
and using a murex shell as a bit, bridles the pair,
spectacular creatures both, that Tethys had bred up together,
gorgeous, fast, and smart. Thetis commands them to wait
in the hip-deep bay while she fetches the sleeping youth from his
         couch
and bears him tenderly down to the beach, limp in her arms.
The waters are still so as not to awaken the huge child
she cradles in her arms. The moonlight shows her the path
that leads to the shore. Close behind, Chiron has followed
to stand on the shingle and, hiding his tears that well in the darkness,
wave his arms in farewell. They whirl away and are gone,   230

leaving only a churned wake of foam on the dark
water. The centaur turns back to the looming shape of the mountain
where now a light breeze has come up to rustle the leaves that sigh
as though the slopes of Othrys and Pholoë grieved together
for him who would come no more to run on their paths and sing
in the joy of his youth. The place was older, sadder. The nymphs
who had watched the beautiful youngster come into manhood
          sorrowed
for none of them now could hope that he might one day choose her.
        The stars in the sky are fading, and Apollo's resplendent car
240 has broken the ocean's surface, sluicing salt water. His steeds
shine in the freshness of morning with droplets of brine. But Thetis,
long gone, has already braved the waves to Scyros'
secluded shore, where she sets the weary dolphins loose.
The young Achilles' eyes flutter. He stirs and wakes,
startled to see how the world is different. The mountains he knows,
Pelion's towering shape, familiar, reliable . . . gone!
Instead, there is all that blue water with glinting waves.
What's happened? Is this a dream? Is this his mother or some
oneiric figment? She reaches her hand to his troubled brow
250 and soothes him, reassuring, "If I had married a god,
I shouldn't have to worry on your behalf or take
these strange precautions. But you are mortal, and death lurks
everywhere, and I worry—all the time, but these days
are worse now than any I've seen. There is danger afloat
in the very air we breathe. But I have devised a plan
by which I may keep you safe. I beg you not to dismiss it
out of hand, but remember how Hercules himself
sat with Omphale's women in Lydia, spinning wool.
Think how Bacchus once put on once a gold-embroidered
260 robe. Or, better, consider how Jupiter tricked himself out
as Diana to fool Callisto. There's nothing inherently wrong
with wearing women's clothing. Caenis was first a girl
and then turned into a man, an especially valiant fighter
as I recall. I entreat you, just for a while, to indulge me.
After the danger is past, I shall restore you to Chiron

and you shall explore again those hills and defiles you have learned
to love, but now, for me, for a little while, I ask you
to do this thing: stay here. When I dipped you into the Styx,
I ought to have done it better . . . " But his face is turned away.
He cannot look at his mother and will not watch as she begs him   270
to do what his pride would never permit him even to think of.
She sees his reluctance and tries a different tack. "No one,"
she reassures him, "will ever know. It will be our secret,
I swear to you." But still it isn't working. Thetis
is growing desperate. She thinks of the boy as an untamed horse
young and full of spirit, resisting the feel of the bridle,
and afraid it means the end of the meadows and pastures he loves,
the end of freedom, and snorts with rage that the heart of a breaker
of horses breaks to hear, but he wears the bridle of fate,
himself, and what can he do? The mother, torn, was desperate,   280
looking about her for help, or up to the heavens where gods
smile or frown on our efforts. Whatever aid she could get
she was eager to have—and it chanced at this moment, the people
        of Scyros
were holding a festival honoring Pallas, their patroness, goddess,
among other things, of seashores. On this particular day,
Lycomedes' daughters emerged from their cloistered life in the
        palace,
their hair woven with blossoms, and carrying flower-decked spears
to welcome with dancing and singing the coming of spring. Achilles
could not help but notice this parade, appearing from nowhere,
of gorgeous, newly nubile girls, all dazzling beauties,   290
making their ceremonial way at the high-water line
sea-wrack traced on the beach. But one among them was special,
outstanding as Venus must be among her nymphs, or Diana
surrounded by beautiful naiads the goddess' looks put to shame.
So does this Deidamia outdazzle her lovely sisters.
It isn't just her figure, her face, complexion, or hair,
but the jewels she wears gleam brighter, the gold of her bracelets
        shines
richer . . . She can't be human. A goddess, perhaps, who has doffed

her helmet and put her regalia aside for the moment? The lad,
300 for all his strength, is undone. He has never before felt passion's
pang within him. Spellbound, dumbfounded he stares,
and, although there's a gentle wind on the beach this moderate
          morning,
there are beads of sweat on his face and body. It is not illness,
for he feels fine, better than he can remember ever
before in his whole life. At once, he is pale and flushed,
the color of milk and blood that Massagetae mix
together and drink or, say, of ivory dyed purple
for odd artistic effects. He would rush forward, abruptly
interrupt their procession, and tell her . . . He doesn't know what
310 in the world he would say. With his mother standing there, he feels
shame and confusion. A young bullock whose curving horns
have not yet fully grown will look at a snowy heifer
and foam at the mouth and cavort in high spirits and yet
not understand what it is that nature is prompting. The herdsmen,
approving, study his antics but guard against what he may do.
So, with Achilles then, and his mother, seizing the moment,
asked him, "Is it so bad to join with those maidens and dance
and sport where they do, and wear those clothes? Do I demand
too much?" He is hardly paying attention as she goes on
320 to inquire whether on Pelion's flanks or Ossa's attractions
are greater than this. She is thinking aloud how fine it would be
to hold in her arms another infant Achilles, a baby
her own baby might give her. He blushes a deeper crimson.
His mother's absurd and undignified plan is no longer out
of the question. To join those girls and always thus to be near her . . .
He cannot resist. Thetis unfolds the dress and throws it
over his head. He lowers his neck to allow the garment
to settle onto his shoulders. Complaisant, he lets her comb
his hair into a gamine's page-boy cut and to deck
330 his neck with a pretty choker. He allows her to play with the skirt
to see that it falls just right. He is even willing to learn
how to walk, how to move his hips as a woman would do.
He lowers his eyes, a demure demoiselle. He is into the game now,

playing as well as he can, as he always does any game.
Like wax under the artist's thumb, he takes the imprint
of what she imposes. She turns her boy to a butch girl
with rather chiseled but all the more attractive features.
  She has him walk down the beach and criticizes his gait
so he doesn't overdo it. She doesn't want him to camp.
She tells him how to hold his arms, what to do with his hands.   340
It's the king he has to fool, or he'll never be admitted
into the women's quarters, where she wants to hide him and he
is now willing and eager to go. She adjusts the bodice,
fluffing it out here and there. Diana, come back from a hunt,
would look more or less like this—slightly disheveled, but gorgeous,
full of that vigor and health outdoorsy women can have.
  It's show time! She takes her son to Lycomedes and presents him:
"Here, oh king, is Achilles' sister, proud in spirit,
an Amazon, one might say. She spurns the idea of marriage.
Let her stay with your daughters who'll teach her maidenly ways.   350
She can help carry their baskets of flowers and fruit to the altars.
It's as much as I can manage to see to Achilles; the girl
needs a different kind of attention, quiet, indoors and secluded.
Most of all, I ask you to keep her away from the harbor
and out of sight of the ships. The sea isn't safe anymore,
and having heard the stories of Paris and what his crew
of Trojans did in Mycenae, I know you'll agree with me: caution
is what we parents must learn." The king has no cause to suspect
the words Thetis has spoken. A mere mortal, he cannot
see through a goddess' wiles. He extends his hand and gives thanks   360
that she has seen fit to trust him. He welcomes the girl and forthwith
sends her to meet the other young ladies with whom she will live.
They look at her as they would at any newcomer—a tall,
broad-shouldered girl, she seems, the field-hockey-captain type.
They invite her, nevertheless, to join their ranks and offer
to teach her the steps of the dances they do in their holy processions.
Think of a flock of doves at Venus' shrine at Idalium,
and how, when a new bird appears, the others at first are cautious
but then settle down and welcome the stranger into their group,

370　flying about her closer and closer until they let her
　　　come with them into their nest to find an opportune perch.
　　　　Thetis watches a while, to see how Achilles performs.
　　　Then, on the pretext of saying good-bye, she speaks in his ear,
　　　words of advice, hints, suggestions, and warnings. At last,
　　　when there's nothing more she can think of, she gives him the
　　　　　quick kiss
　　　a mother would give a daughter and plunges into the sea.
　　　As she swims, she looks back at the island to bless it and offer
　　　prayers that the place she has hidden her child may prosper in safety
　　　and silence, as Crete kept silent for Rhea when she gave birth there
380　to Jove. She thinks how the wandering island of Delos earned
　　　honor and shrines, and she hopes for such an outcome for Scyros—
　　　that the winds and waves may revere it, the Nereids all may play there,
　　　and ships seeking a refuge from the sudden Aegean storms
　　　may find in its lee their haven . . . except for the keels of the Greeks
　　　who may come in search of Achilles. "Let there be balmy breezes
　　　of peace where the Bacchic thyrsus is the closest thing to a weapon.
　　　Let terrible Mars who rages and rants roam where he will
　　　throughout the world, but keep him far from this hole in the corner
　　　where Achilles romps and primps with the princesses' companions."
390　　　At the same time, in Greece, there is talk of the outrage—
　　　complaints,
　　　entreaties, and threats. The speeches resound in the council
　　　　chambers.
　　　Agamemnon's ambassadors argue how his brother's wife's
　　　　disappearance,
　　　a sneaky business, at night, perpetrated by cowards
　　　afraid to fight in a proper battle, was all the more
　　　outrageous, offensive, insulting, an affront not to be borne
　　　by men of honor. A daughter of Jove is taken away?
　　　No woman in Greece can think of herself as safe. No man
　　　can be sure, at the break of dawn, that the wife he loves will be there
　　　to greet the new day with him. If foreign raiders commit
400　such crimes as this, the assault is on sovereignty itself.
　　　If a king's wife can be taken, what may the commons expect?

The harmony of the nations is at stake here. The basic beliefs
and assumptions of civilization are called into question. These men,
or, say, these less-than-human, Asiatic vermin,
have got to be taught a lesson! And so on, and on and on,
the words are spoken from one end of Greece to the other, and words
soon enough give way to different, more earnest sounds of work
in the Cypriot mines, for example, in Temasus for the copper
they'll need to make the bronze for weapons. All of Euboea
resounds with the ringing of axes and shipwrights' adzes. Mycenae   410
gasps and clangs as the smithies' bellows work in their forges
and the workmen pound on their anvils. From every part of the
          country,
weapons are coming, and carts, and the hides of beasts for shields
and quivers to carry the arrows. The harvest is also of men,
platoons, companies, regiments coming together to fight,
foot soldiers, of course, but cavalry too, and the horses,
enormous numbers of horses from Epirus' upland meadows.
Into the shadowy groves of Boeotia and Phocis, there comes
an unaccustomed light as the woodsmen thin the trees
for javelin shafts and oars. Iron forges are working   420
day and night to produce rough coats of mail for the soldiers,
hames and bits for the horses, and armor for vessels' prows.
In the fiery glow where smiths are heating and pounding metal,
you can see the color of blood those weapons will soon be drinking,
and hear in the rasp of the whetstone on the edges of spears and
          swords
the râles of dying men. The craftsmen are bending the wood
to form the bowmen's weapons, pounding the helmet vizors,
and fixing the gaudy plumage onto their crests. All Greece
is a hive with a swarm of workers buzzing in sinister menace.
Only in Thessaly people haven't the least idea   430
to whom to turn for a leader: Peleus now is too old,
and Achilles far too young. (In any event, where is he?)
     The Peloponessus assembles its horses, equipment, and men
who put to sea, and their neighbors, the other Greek kingdoms,
          mainland

and island people, are making their way to converge in a mighty
armada at sacred Aulis. The panoply of their mainsails
spreads out on the blue of the sea and swallows the wind's breath.
At the southern end of Euboea, there at the promontory
in the place Diana delights to roam near the rocky cliffs
440   where Mount Caphareus juts into the water, the fleet
heaves to. The Greeks make camp and swear allegiance
and Troy's destruction. It is something to see, a marvel, an orderly
jumble of men with their arms and baggage. Sometimes on hunts,
when the beaters and wielders of nets are driving the quarry,
         shouting,
waving their burning torches, and banging drums, the beasts
will flock to the narrow defile to which they are being prompted,
stag and boar and bear and wolf and lion together,
puzzled at how their range on the mountainside has shrunk,
and reconciled for the time by their common fear of the men
450   from whom they are fleeing. So are the various Greeks united.
     Joined with the sons of Atreus is Diomedes, the son
of Tydeus—with him is Sthenelus who drives his dreadnaught car.
Antilochus also is there with his father, aged Nestor.
Ajax has come, bearing a shield made from the hides
of seven enormous bullocks. Ulysses too has arrived
and is full of plans and intricate schemes to further the cause,
but they all agree they need Achilles. The name of Achilles
is everywhere spoken, the echo of its bearer's immanent absence.
Who else can fight against Hector? Who else can threaten the
         haughty
460   tower of Troy and its king, defiant Priam? They tell
stories of how, as a baby, Achilles learned to crawl
in the mountain passes from which the snow had barely been
         cleared.
Who else was reared by a centaur from early childhood? Who
can claim a better line of descent, with his mother a goddess
who took him down to the Styx and dipped his limbs in its water
to make his flesh like armor, proof against any steel?
These stories and others they tell from tent to tent, and the camp

is gloomy indeed, for the chieftains admit there is not his like
anywhere in the world. They need him. Ages ago,
it must have been like this when the gods and the giants fought   470
on Phlegra's fields. Mars brandished his Thracian spear;
Minerva roiled her nest of deadly vipers; Apollo
bent his enormous bow; and the world waited in terror
for the needed one to appear—Jove with his thunder and lightning.
When would he come? Would he bring with him the mighty
       weapons
from Aetna's bowels without which there was little hope of winning?
  There are consultations and formal discussions, as well as
       impromptu
mutterings, protests, and even accusations. The mood
is not good. While the princes adjourn and reconvene,
the troops watch and wait, wondering when they will sail,   480
or whether they'll sail at all. Then, in a public quarrel,
the fiery Protesilaus, eager to fight though aware
that he has been fated to die, the first of the Greek host,
dares to rebuke the prophet Calchas, son of Thestor:
"You call yourself a priest of Apollo and carry that tripod
on which to offer the god his sacrifices, but you
do not put to our use your gifts of prophecy. Speak,
in the name of the god, now that we need his hidden wisdom.
You hear the incessant clamor for Achilles to come and join us.
Diomedes is here, but that doesn't count with the people.   490
And Telemonian Ajax, and the Locrian Ajax as well
are here with us. But the men seem unimpressed, ungrateful,
and call out for this other fighter they seem to adore
as if he were some god of war. Very well then. Let us
have him. Your hair is wreathed with the prophet's garland. Tell us
where he hides, along what coast? Of what sea? Declare
where we should look! Our scouts tell us he's left the cave
of Chiron. And no one in Thessaly in king Peleus' palace
has any idea where he skulks. Do whatever you do
to rouse the god from his slumber. Drink the potion, burn   500
the incense, recite the spells, and perform. You do not wear

the armor of fighting men and are safe from the wounds of war
that may not profane your sacred person; for this you bear
a different kind of burden. We shall do you honor as great
as we do our greatest chiefs if you will but tell us where
in the wide world to look to find the mighty Achilles."
    Calchas looks around him, ashen pale. Is he angry?
He rolls his eyes and makes a series of spastic gestures.
A frenzy it is, a fit, a sign of the god's attendance,
510 or say, rather, possession. Calchas seems deaf and blind
and altogether senseless as he heeds the words of the god
that rise up out of the tripod's smoke from its smoldering laurel.
The hair streams out from his head, and he looks quite mad as he
    moans,
but then those moans begin to acquire the shapes of words:
"Where?" he asks and again, "Where?" drawing out the single
syllable on the air, where it floats. "Where have you gone?
Where have you taken Chiron's pupil? Send him back!
He is mine! You are a goddess, Thetis, but I speak
for Apollo, and you cannot stash him away while Asia awaits
520 his rough embrace. I see her. I see him! I see the sea,
a beach, an island, far away. I see Lycomedes' face!
I see Achilles . . . wearing a woman's gown. Oh, rip it,
rip it off, and ignore your mother's disgraceful fears.
I see other women, wicked, and hear their erotic giggles . . .
He is lost, lost . . . " And the raving and tottering stops. He
    shudders
and then goes limp and collapses in a heap before the altar.
    Diomedes turns to Ulysses and under their breath they confer:
"It's us, isn't it? You and me? Who else would go?
Your choice, of course. But should you decide to do it, I'm with you.
530 You will find him, wherever he is, wherever he's gone
to ground—or water, as like as not. There's no one smarter,
even without that prophet's ambiguous help." Ulysses
thinks for a while and agrees: "It's a job of work, I grant you.
But what if we try and fail? It won't look good, and the camp
will be worse off then than it is right now. We shall be disgraced!

And yet . . . If we don't even try, that doesn't look good." He
    pauses.
"We can always shift the blame," he says blandly, "to Calchas."
    So they volunteer. The Greeks applaud, and great Agamemnon
makes one of his fulsome speeches on difficulty and courage.
Then, like a flock of birds coming home to roost in the evening,   540
wheeling all together, or, say, like a swarm of bees
returning at night to the hive, the troops make way for the two
heroes who march together to the waiting ship on the beach.
The sails, unfurled, belly out to catch the wind as the oarsmen
row with a will. The ship is away. They are off and running.
    And back at the Scyros zenana? By this time, Deidamia
has learned the delicious truth—that the new girl isn't a girl
but a man. Do her sisters know? She can't be sure. If they do,
they pretend, out of fear or politeness, not to have noticed a thing.
The moment Achilles' mother departed, this bashful and shy   550
creature turned more outgoing. He took the princess' hand
and held it tight in a strong, not at all maidenly grip.
Picking her out as his special friend? Well, young girls do that.
But those eyes follow her always. He's never away from her side.
He teases her, flinging blossoms or whole garlands of flowers,
and it's more than friendship. A girlish crush? That often happens,
but this is different. He plays the lyre for her and shows her
how to make interesting chords. He puts his hands upon hers
to demonstrate how, and his touch lingers gently, sweetly.
He holds her close and kisses her, hard . . . He's hardly a girl!   560
No doubt now. He confesses what she now knows for sure,
and tells her who he is, and putting it into a song,
recounts the details of his birth and childhood. She in her turn
helps him with his imposture, teaching him how to move,
sit, speak, spin, and maintain the pretense on which
their staying together, hour by hour and day by day,
depends. And yet, she wonders why he has picked her out
from all the girls. How deep is his love? Would it not be better
if they weren't to stay so close? For the sake of keeping their secret,
but also to see what he does, how long he will wait, and how patient   570

his love can be, she avoids him. It's a game she plays, that they both
play, but in greater earnest than girlish games. She thinks
of Jove on Olympus and how that god and his sister, Juno,
must at a certain moment have romped this way, as their innocent
sport turned suddenly real, and the sister and brother became,
as if by a change of light and despite the taboo, lovers.

    Her thought reaches out to a similar thought, as a body yearns
for another body. The wiles of Thetis are working too well.
In a sacred grove, the women of Scyros, every three years,

580   go to celebrate Bacchus' mystic rites, to dance,
sing, and feel that frenzy in which the god takes delight.
By law and custom, no male is allowed to set foot on that holy
ground. The king has thus commanded, and, keeping watch,
an aged priestess prevents any would-be interlopers
from daring to come too close. Achilles finds this amusing
and laughs to himself—his companions cannot imagine why.
He leads the parade of maidens, moving his arms like a willowy
girl, and it's more than plausible. The ceremonial nebris
of fawn skin hangs from his neck with ivy wound in its folds.

590   His hair is done up with a purple ribbon. He wields the sacred
thyrsus as if he has trained for years to perform this way.
Deidamia once was the fairest of all, but now
Peleus' splendid child and Thetis' seems just as fair.
One thinks of the god for whom they perform these rites, of
      Bacchus
who managed, when the occasion required, somehow to put on
not only the paraphernalia of fighting but even the look,
the angry brow and the sternly jutting jaw for his war
on the Indian tribes. Just so, or inversely so, Achilles
was tamed and gentled now, disarmed and quite disarming.

600   Darkness fell, and the moon arose in its silver car
to reign in the dome of heaven. Sleep with his gentle wings
gathered the world below in feathers of blessed silence.
The songs of the women hushed to the notes of memory's score,
and their metal gongs were mute, encased in the velvet blackness.
Achilles got up and wandered a little way from the group

to stand alone and consider the thoughts of his troubled mind.
"Is this how I spend my life?" he accused himself. "My manhood
wastes away in this pillowed prison. My mother's fears
have sapped my strength. I imagine running, hunting down beasts,
and my hands that would grasp spearshafts and sword hilts clench
    upon air.   610
I think of those mountain paths my feet remember so clearly.
Do they perhaps miss me? Do the mountains wonder where
their careless boy has gone? Are the streams and pools I swam in
different now? Do they all suppose I am dead? I am
halfway there, in this life that is no man's life. I float
in a dream of my mother's devising, and would rouse myself but
    cannot.
Does Chiron mourn for the ghost I have all but become? Does
    Patroclus,
as he bends my bow and shoots my arrows, sometimes think
of that comrade he once knew and of where he is now? I spin
wool with women! Shame! But a virile spirit rebels.   620
I play at love, but even there, it's a children's game,
another source of chagrin and self-reproach. My manhood
is utterly gone, denied, undone. And yet I may find it."
    So, in the silent gloom, he debates with himself and discovers
the inner truth of his nature and being, which one must admit
or else, by denial, forfeit. He tiptoes back to the group,
finds the girl in the darkness, and takes her by force, his desire
the master now of both fates, hers and his own. The stars
look down in chilly candor on what had been foreordained,
and the horns of the moon blush red, as if some poet or painter   630
has designed the scene to let nature demonstrate what the gods
themselves know in their hearts of the actions of men and women.
Deidamia cries out—in fear and pain? Or in pleasure?
The grove rings with her rhythmic keening the hillside echoes,
and on every side the women awake. They take it as sign
that one of their number has been possessed somehow by the god
they have come to the grove to worship. They rise and join in, their
    shouts

a chorus of squeals in soprano, contralto moans, and cries
no one could place on a scale. Achilles holds the girl
640   in his close embrace and assures her as best he can, "It's me,"
he whispers, "the one you love, Achilles, the son of immortal
Thetis. Only for you did I put on a woman's clothing.
To be with you, whom I loved the moment I saw you. For you
I learned to spin and sew and how to walk like a lady.
Why do you weep? You are Thetis' daughter-in-law. Be brave
and even proud, for you bring forth a great-grandson of almighty
Jove himself. You have nothing to fear, I promise. Your father's
royal anger, is it? I shall destroy his city
with fire and sword, will leave no stone upon a stone,
650   before I let him punish his daughter for my misdeed.
I will protect you, I promise," he says again and again
as he strokes her hair. The girl is horrified, in shock,
and yet she is able to listen, and, just as important, to think
of what she can do. Report this crime to her father? Ruin,
for everyone, for her father, herself, and . . . her lover, too!
Does she want him dead? Would his death undo what he has done?
Has she not already imagined how this might one day happen
and dreamed with happy anticipation of how it would be?
Not this way, but still, it has happened. She tells herself
660   she loves him, but what does that mean? She does not try to speak
but thinks of the general sadness of how things are in the world.
At length she decides, and tells him they share the guilt together.
She will be silent. They'll keep their secret, confide in no one
except her nurse whom she trusts with her life. That kindly woman
promises she will help them, and does, and they keep it quiet—
the rape and its result that she carries now in her womb.
Weeks go by, and months, and Lucina, goddess of childbirth,
appears when the time is ripe to preside at the birth of the baby.

But now, in the offing, Ulysses' ship, which has threaded its way
670   among the Aegean islands, is tacking one way and another,
through the Cyclades, past Paros, Olearos, and Lemnos.
They have left Naxos behind, and Samos. Delos' shape

has shadowed their craft while the sailors poured out over the
　　transom
libations of wine to the god in prayer that Apollo's priest,
undeceived, was speaking the truth. Did the great god hear them?
Apparently so, for a wind came up from the heights of Cynthus
to belly the sail in fortunate omen and speed their journey
across the water. The gods or the fates were decided, and Thetis
could not alone gainsay them or reverse their stern decrees.
Apollo could see for himself, looking back from his car　　　　680
that now hung low in the sky, its rays blazing the water
into crazed and glittering streams, that the ship was nearing Scyros,
and Thetis, who tried to roil the waves, bestir the winds,
and rouse the savage elements against that baleful boat,
was impotent, terrified, a part of an ongoing nightmare
in which her will was frozen and her voice stilled. She watched
that wake spread out behind the stern like a sluggish arrow.
　　The other gods and goddesses looked on—Pallas, for instance,
the keeper of Scyros' shore—as the Argives approached,
　　disembarked,
and offered prayers of thanks. The Ithacan hero is shrewd　　　690
and, lest he alarm the locals, orders the crew to remain
on the beach. Diomedes and he will make their way to the castle
and announce themselves. In the tower, keeping watch, a servant,
Abas, has already seen them. He runs to the council chamber
with news that a Greek ship has appeared in the harbor. The two
chiefs follow the obvious path up the hill. They seem
harmless enough. One thinks of a pair of desperate wolves
who have teamed together to feed themselves and their hungry cubs,
and, looking like stray dogs, slink along toward the sheepfold.
　　Diomedes, who's none too bright, wants to know the plan.　　700
He has no idea how they'll find Achilles or why Ulysses
told him to bring all those combs, brooches, knick-knacks,
　　gew-gaws,
scarves, and little religious objects. How will it work?
Ulysses, with half his attention, explains the not very subtle
trick he has figured out. What he's thinking about himself

is how he signed on to be part of an epic and now is playing
his role in a farce—how strange are the tastes of the heavenly gods!
"The trinkets," he says, "are bait. If Achilles is trying to hide
among Lycomedes' women, we'll use these toys to catch him,
710 these and the fancy shield with the carving and gold chasings,
and the good spear. Bring that, and tell Agyrtes to come,
with his bugle hidden away but ready to sound an alarm
when I give him the signal." Again and again, he runs over the plan.
   They approach the gate of the castle where the old king
     awaits them,
surrounded by his court and they in turn by guards.
Ulysses holds out before him the branch of an olive in token
of peaceful intentions. He bows and addresses Lycomedes: "News
has reached your ears, O king, of the war of Europe with Asia.
The world has called the roll of the names of the mighty chieftains,
720 which even here must echo on the tranquil island air.
Beside me is Diomedes, Tydeus' son, even greater
than was his most excellent sire; I am Ulysses, king
of Ithaca; we come here, I am frank to say, to discover,
among the approaches to Troy whose shore we aim for, the best,
the safest, the least expected . . . What are their preparations?
What are their plans? What movements of ships and men have
     you seen?"
It was not clear that he'd finished, but the King of Scyros broke in
with words of welcome: "I pray the gods may favor your cause!
Your visit does honor to me and my house. I welcome you here."
730 He leads them inside the gate, through the courtyard, and into
     the hall
where attendants prepare the couches and feasting tables. Ulysses
looks this way and that, approving, admiring, also
observing to see if one girl might be taller than others or marked
with somewhat masculine features. He wanders about like a tourist,
noting the castle's decor, its setting, its views of the hills,
but all the time he is scouting . . . Think of a hound in a field
that roves one way and another, alert for a movement, a scent,
some track of the quarry he seeks, nearby and perhaps unawares.

But the quarry knows. The zenana is all atwitter. The girls
can speak of nothing else—a ship of the Greeks has arrived,   740
and the king has welcomed the strangers, invited them in, and
     guests
from all over the island are coming, decked in their finest,
to dine with the VIPs. There's excitement and some apprehension—
one never knows what strangeness strangers bring with them.
     But one
is nothing less than joyous: Achilles knows why they're here
and recognizes his moment. Whatever may happen, the time
for which he has waited so long has come, and now at last
he can feel he is living his life. He can't stay away, but adventures
into the hall for a look at the guests who recline on the fancy
couches, drinking, nibbling dainties, and being seen.   750
Indeed, the king has commanded the ladies come to him now,
the princess and all her attendants. Like an Amazon army, they
     troop,
descending upon the room with predictable girlish noise.
as Ulysses figures the odds: does the king not know? Or is this
a clever demonstration that he's hiding nothing and no one
here in the palace? The guest inspects the girls—who wouldn't?—
but it's hard to see by the light of the oil lamps and smoking
     torches.
Still, there is one who arouses Ulysses' suspicion . . . tall?
Not so shy as the others? A trick of the light? Or is there
something truly different about that one at the end?   760
He nudges his companion and nods at the one he means,
raising a questioning brow. But then—is it quite by chance?—
Deidamia blocks their view. The two girls whisper secrets,
are perfectly innocent maybe. Or maybe not. The tall one
seems about to stand up, but the other shakes her finger
and goes to fetch more wine. Later Ulysses glances
and notes how the prettiest daughter is smoothing the other's hair
and adjusting her golden headband. But the servants bring more
     food
and then, when the tables are cleared and more wine is poured,

770   the king gets up to speak, to toast the Achaeans, pledge
his loyalty, and confess his envy of their great chance.
"Were I of the proper age for such undertakings, I'd go,
join with you to fight, as I used to be able to do.
The Dolopians came to Scyros, attacked us . . . The wrecks of
     their ships,
those overturned keels on the beach, are monuments now to that
     battle.
Their arms are up there on display on the castle walls. But now
I'm past all that. Too old, I can't even offer sons.
And none of my daughters as yet has provided me with
     grandsons . . . "
At this point, Ulysses rises, seizes the moment, and answers,
780   looking from time to time at that large girl down the table:
"I thank you, sir, and believe in your words—for who would not
     yearn
to join with us, to be part of this glorious venture? The chiefs
and princes of Greece have assembled on the field of honor.
     The power
of Europe has come together, united, strong, and determined
to do what is right. Our cities are all but empty. Our fields
have given their beasts and our forests are stripped for hulls
     and masts.
Fish look up from their depths to a surface dark with our vessels,
as birds look down to the sea's patchwork blanket of sails.
Fathers present their sons with heirloom weapons the younger
790   hands seize, and they're gone, in an instant. Never before
has bravery had such a chance to earn renown and glory,
and never before has the fighting skill of our best had occasion
in which to display itself in so just a cause." He looks
from face to face as he watches his words take their toll like blows
on the anvils of their souls. Some eyes are avoiding his.
The men of Scyros stare down at the floor beneath their places
as the Ithacan prince winds up with his usual peroration:
"Whoever has noble blood that flows in his veins, whoever
has known the pride of his javelin's hitting the target truly,

whoever is good with horses, or the skill of the bow, or can offer   800
excellence, valor, and virtue, your moment has come. This war
awaits you with mighty names that will sound in the mouths of men
forever!" But then he puts in a new line or two. "Your mothers'
fears cannot hold you at home, or the arms of sweethearts who hate
the glory that you, deep in your heart, have always longed for."
And, yes, that girl he's been watching seems to be trying to rise.
To agree? To volunteer? It is hard to tell, for the women
all get up and together withdraw from the hall. Ulysses
watches as that one lingers behind a moment, but then
is gone with the rest. He turns to the men and concludes his   810
      remarks:
"I wish you well. I hope your daughters may all find husbands
worthy of their great beauty and charm." Then he sits down
and asks about the girl he saw at the end of the table.
The king is pleased by Ulysses' interest. "Aren't they pretty
each and every one? If the winds keep you here for a while,
perhaps you may wish tomorrow to observe them perform the rites
of Bacchus or those of Pallas." Ulysses is quick to accept
this kind invitation. And so to bed, but during the long
hours of night, he remains awake. He is endlessly thinking,
considering ways it could happen, and eager for dawn to break,   820
as of course, at last, it does. At first light, as arranged,
Diomedes is coming up from the ship, and with him Agyrtes,
and the chest full of presents. At length the young women
assemble to perform their dances and reels for the guests.
Leading this grand cotillion are the princess Deidamia
and the one to whom Ulysses was paying special attention
the evening before at dinner. The music of pan-pipes trills
and the cymbals of Cybele crash, as the drums beat faster and faster,
while the girls perform their intricate elegant steps. They raise
and lower their wands and the ribbons float on the air as is done   830
in Samothrace and Crete in that complicated series
of geometrical figures they trace in their performance.
Ulysses notes that the girl he has spotted is . . . not very good,
seems not to know the steps, not even really to care,

as if this entire performance is somehow a joke. Achilles
makes mistakes, and laughs, clumps and lumbers, moves
in a parody of dancing, a skeptic, an unbeliever,
a Pentheus come from Thebes to watch the Bacchantes perform
(and the women in their frenzy tore him limb from limb).
840   At last they are done and the girls acknowledge the guests' polite
applause and gather around the hall table where presents
are out on display. Diomedes invites them to choose what they will.
They look to the king who is pleased and nods in assent—he cannot
suppose that the gifts of Greeks are not always what they may seem.
He has, in any event, no cause to suspect Ulysses,
famed though he is for his guile. The girls, being girls, are attracted
to the little drums and ritual cymbals, or pretty headbands
set with precious stones. To the weapons they pay no mind,
or else they assume these are gifts for Lycomedes himself,
850   but the bold Achilles, Peleus' son, of Aeacus' line,
is dazzled. His eyes shine at the sheen of the gold on that shield.
The wonderful workmanship invites him. The battle scenes
on the boss and around the rim speak to his spirit. He lifts
the shield and the spear beside it, hefts them, wields them,
        wears them
as the soul wears its flesh. He forgets his mother's instructions
and Deidamia's hints. He plants his feet like a soldier
and tries one battle cry that rings out from the stonework.
His eyes are ablaze and his hair is electric, an animal's hackles . . .
Think of a lion cub that some hunter has reared and tamed,
860   a regular pussycat, but then one day, when it sees
the steel of the javelin's tip, something deep in its heart
rebels. The beast reverts, goes wild, ashamed to have fawned
and purred and played like a pet. It turns on its keeper and mauls him.
The room is hushed. They are all staring. Achilles puts down
the shield, but he sees in the metal his own reflection—a face
noble and warlike, but wearing a woman's headband and earrings.
He is thrilled and he blushes in shame. He cannot move. Ulysses
already beside him is speaking calmly, one man to another:
"We know who you are. But more important, you know.

The game is over. The ship is waiting. The moment is here.　870
The towering walls of Troy invite you. At every step
you take in their direction, they tremble. You did as your mother
instructed, but now it's over." Ulysses removes the headband
from Achilles' head and looks to Agyrtes, who takes the trumpet
from the folds of his cloak and blows it, a piercing martial blast
that scatters the terrified girls. But Achilles, strange to believe,
grows taller, broader . . . Amazing! He towers over Ulysses.
That spear in his huge hand now seems like a mere toy
as he waits, poised, ready for Hector or anyone else.
　　There's confusion, even panic. What's happened to Peleus'　880
daughter?
From the next room Deidamia, hearing that war cry, hurries,
knowing that all is lost, but hoping somehow to retrieve
what she can. Achilles sees her, hears her drawn-out wail
of grief, and is undone. He drops the spear and shield
that clatter onto the flagstones and he turns to face the king,
who is utterly mystified. "I apologize, your highness.
I am that daughter Thetis entrusted to your safekeeping.
It is fated—always was—that yours be the house from which
I should proceed to Troy. Whatever I do there shall surely
redound to both our honors, and Chiron's as well," he says.　890
The king is stunned, and Achilles presses on: "To this news,
I add a further detail. The goddess Thetis brought you
her child, and I leave behind a child—her grandson and yours."
There is no response. Achilles continues, "I ask for your daughter's
hand, that we may consecrate what has been consummated.
Mine is a worthy house, royal and divine, and fit
to join with yours. You approve, I trust. Or if you cannot,
then let all the blame be mine. Your daughter could not resist
the embrace of these strong arms." The king's mouth gapes as
　　Achilles
asks for pardon and places, at the foot of the throne, his baby.　900
"Would you put your daughter to death, and me, and this, your
　　grandson,
all at once?" Ulysses and all the Greeks kneel down

as suppliants, and the king is helpless. All these people,
and behind them, casting greater shadows, the fates, the gods,
are bullying him to submit, as he does. What option is there?
What else can he possibly do? He thinks of his promise to Thetis,
but, at last, he nods. His daughter gazes at him with love
and then turns to Achilles—his son-in-law now, Achilles!
The king sees her take the hero's hand in her hand.

910   Details, details. At once, a courier hurries off
to Peleus' court on the mainland, to inform him of these events,
and to ask his blessing, and also ships and men to go
with Achilles to Troy. For his part, Lycomedes offers vessels,
two ships with their crews and fighting men. He is deeply
sorry he cannot give more to the cause. There is drinking and
        feasting
to celebrate all: the alliance, the wedding, the birth, the great
day which draws to its close. As night comes on, the lovers
retire, no longer furtive, for their last night together. Forever?
    She has no idea. She is worried, can see in her mind's eye

920 Xanthus' sinuous banks and Ida's lofty crest
and imagine the dreadful things that will happen there when
        the Greek
ships have reached that shore. She lies in the dark, afraid
of the dawn's approach. She can feel the minutes oozing away
and, with arms around her lover's neck, she weeps as she asks him,
"Will I ever see you again? Will we lie together in bed
the way we are now? Will you see your infant son grown up
to boyhood and manhood? Or will you go straight home
from Troy to Thessaly, passing this little island by
where you once wore a maiden's clothing? For months I waited
        for this,

930 for us to be joined as man and wife, but now my dream
has come cruelly true, for we have but this single night
and then you are gone. It's hard as well for you, I know,
and my misery makes it worse, but what can I do? Our love
deserves better than this but must perforce give way
to the needs of the time. You must go. I realize that, and I fret

that Thetis was right to fear what may happen there. Go, then,
but try to be careful. Try to come back to me. I wish you
more luck than a soldier's wife should dare to hope for.
Go and come back. The Trojan women will sigh and swoon,
eager to be your slaves and concubines. Your couch   940
will seem to them more alluring than their own Trojan beds.
Helen herself will be tempted to come down one night to your
        tent . . .
Which do I hate worse? Will you entertain your pals
with stories about your conquest in Scyros? Or will you forget
we ever met? It's dreadful but . . . Why can't I go with you
to Troy, dressed as a man, as you dressed here as a girl?"
But she remembers their little baby. "Think of him," she insists,
"of the two of us here together, and . . . grant me this one
        request—
let none of your trophy women bear you their bastard children,
unworthy grandsons to Thetis and half-brothers to our   950
dear child . . . " Achilles is moved and he strokes her hair
as he swears his oath that he will come back one day to Scyros
with treasures from Troy, but a breeze just come up from the harbor
carries away his weightless words on the mists of dawn.

Book II

The god of the sun emerges from ocean to strip the world
of the shroud of night. His torch at first is dim, moist
with the brine of the sea, but it soon burns off to reveal clearly
Achilles, his shoulders bare now, that woman's robe thrown down.
The wind that rattles the lines on the spars in the harbor tousles
his hair, eager, prompting a quick departure. He holds
the spear and the shield, and no one who sees him would even dare
compare this image of valor and strength with that other transvestite
figment. It's as though his time on Scyros has never happened.

10   Assume he's departing only now from Chiron's cave. Ulysses
advises the younger hero that the pious and proper thing
would be to propitiate the gods with the lives of beasts.
He agrees, and dedicates a huge bull to the sea-gods,
Neptune, of course, and Nereus, his own grandfather. To Thetis
he gives a spotless heifer with garlands wound on its head,
and, casting the animal's entrails onto the waves, he prays:
"Mother, I did as you told me, hard as it was to obey,
but they found me out, as you see, and they want me to come. They
    need me.
I must go with the Greeks to Troy. Forgive me, protect and help
    me."

20   And then he boards, as the offshore wind picks up to speed
the journey. The island of Scyros dwindles away astern,
a smallish lump in the mist on the wide expanse of sea.
    Far off, on the topmost turret of the castle wall, with her sisters
crowded about her, weeping, his wife looks out at the tiny

sail in the distance. She holds the child in her arms, young Pyrrhus,
and stares. Is that dot that swims in her blurring vision real?
She has no idea but dares not turn her head or blink.
From the deck, Achilles looks back at a toy city, the wall
he thinks he can still make out, and somewhere back there, a
    woman.
He is filled with grief, and Ulysses stands at his side to offer   30
words of comfort and courage: "Is this the man the Greeks
agreed they needed? Is this the man the oracle told us
our cause depends on? The portals of War have opened and we
have already crossed its threshold. Your mother, as fond of you
as she was and as worried on your behalf, ought to have known
it was altogether hopeless to attempt to hide your brave
heart in a woman's clothes. It wasn't the shield or spear,
but that trumpet blast, or rather its resonance deep within you.
Nothing could keep you away, as you knew all along. Do not
blame your mother, or us, or yourself. This is how things are."   40
Achilles understands quite well what the Ithacan chieftain
is trying to do. "My sojourn in Scyros, my woman's clothing . . .
That's all behind us now. Tell me instead the story
of what has happened to bring us to the brink of war and beyond.
Fill my heart," he says, "with the fire of righteous anger."
    "The story begins," says Ulysses, "with a shepherd boy and his
        flock.
But he's not really a shepherd. It's Paris, Hector's brother,
out on the grassy slopes of Ida watching his flock
of pet sheep. By chance, this is the one the goddesses
choose, the three of them needing some impartial mortal   50
to judge who is the fairest." He shakes his head at the strange
way of the world and goes on. "He doesn't pick Minerva
and wisdom, and he doesn't look at Juno and power. This slip
of a lad decides it is Dione's daughter, Venus, and love
that win the prize—the apple, that Eris, the goddess of discord
flung down at your parents' wedding, to which she came
uninvited and therefore determined to do mischief.
The three goddesses quarrel when Paris has made his choice

     as Eris all along intended they should. It was fated,
60   as it also was that you should come to fight in this war.
     Paris claims his bribe—they all offered bribes—from Venus:
     the world's loveliest woman. She happens, of course, to be married,
     but what is that to a goddess? Paris cuts timbers and hews
     planks for a keel and fells a trunk for the mast of a ship
     to sneak into Sparta and kidnap the wife of King Menelaus.
     We soon hear of this outrage, and from all over Greece we gather
     without any urging or prompting or talk of treaties, for vengeance.
     Civilization itself is at stake here. The laws of men
     imply that we are not beasts. If the marriage bond is sacred,
70   then how can we live in honor when a king suffers such insult?
     It isn't a flock of sheep or a herd of oxen he took,
     but a woman, a wife, a queen, and a god's daughter. What man
     could bear such a loss? When King Agenor's daughter, Europa,
     was carried away on the back of a powerful god, did he
     suffer in silence, or go to the ends of the earth in his quest
     for his purloined child? Did Aeëtes sit on his hands when Medea
     ran off with cunning Jason? With ships and men and weapons
     he followed behind them eager for justice and vengeance! Shall we
     endure as grave an affront on the part of this Phrygian fop?
80   Have we lost our horses, weapons, hearts, and honor? Are seas
     that Trojans cross sailing westward closed to us, sailing east?
     How would you feel if some stranger came sneaking ashore at
          Scyros
     to grab your wife, to snatch her from her room in the palace, her
          father's
     love and her child's, as she struggled and cried out in fear and rage,
     'Achilles! Achilles!'?" In reflex, the hero's hand had seized
     the hilt of his sword and already drawn it halfway from its scabbard.
     What more does Ulysses need to say? After several moments,
     Diomedes changes the subject. "Confide in us as your friends
     and tell us about your childhood and how you were reared in the
          centaur's
90   famous and difficult school. What were the stories he told you
     of the ancient heroes' deeds? What did he make you do?

How did he train you in strength, endurance, and skill? In fairness,
and for our exertions, our trouble in coming to fetch you from
    Scyros,
tell us whatever you can of Chiron's wonderful methods."
    No one dislikes talking about himself, but Achilles'
modesty prevents him from appearing to boast. Even so,
having been asked in this way, he feels compelled to respond:
"I started with Chiron early, as an infant really. I'm told
I was never given what children usually eat. He fed me
only when I was extremely hungry, and then he gave me   100
the entrails of lions and wolves for my baby teeth to chew on.
For as long as I can remember, he took me with him whenever
he ventured into the forests. I'd run along beside him
on my little legs and try to keep up with his powerful stride.
I never felt any fear of wild beasts. He taught me
to laugh in delight when I saw them; he gave me a quiver and bow,
and a spear, and I learned the joys of the chase. I lived in the woods,
where I came to know the roar of the waterfalls and the hush
of the empty glade. To the heat of the summer sun, or the bitter
cold of the winter's night, I became accustomed. That other   110
children's lives were different, I had no idea. They slept
on beds that weakened their bodies, but I lay down on the cold
hard ground with my master's flank as my only pillow.
At twelve, I could outrun a deer and bring it down without nets
or packs of hounds to help me. I was faster than any horse—
or even a centaur, for Chiron used to gallop behind me
and tease, and we'd race together over the meadows, running
for miles until I was utterly spent. Then he'd praise my effort
and hoist me up on his back and carry me home. He taught me
how to walk out on new-formed ice of a stream in winter,   120
taking my steps lightly so I didn't break through to get soaked
in the bone-chilling water . . . I thought it was fun to do this,
a game, but there were rules I learned: it wasn't sporting
to go for the gentle doe or the timid lynx. Brave boys
only hunt bears in their caves, or wild boars with their sharp
tusks. I was also permitted lions up in their mountain

lairs, and, I think, tigers—which are rare in this part of the world.
I'd go out on the trails, and Chiron would wait at the cave
to welcome me home, stained with the blood of the beasts and my
        own.
130   He'd look me over, check my bag, and inspect my weapons,
and only then embrace me and patch me up. He was training
my spirit, of course, but he also taught me particular skills.
There was more or less formal drill in the use of Paeonian darts,
and I learned to throw the Macedonian javelin, wield
the Sarmatian pike, the curved sword of the Getans, the huge
Gelonian bow, and the Balearic sling-shot you have to swing
around and around your head as you figure the arc to the target.
Aside from these various weapons, there was also basic training
in jumping, climbing, running, and hand-eye coordination.
140   He'd give me a shield and then throw stones for me to fend off.
He taught me not to inhale as I ran through fires. He made me
stand still, plant myself like a rock, and then come charging
with a team of horses I'd have to grab and stop in their tracks.
Or he'd put me into a river, the Spercheus' rapids, for instance,
when spring rains had it flooded—I'd stand there and fight the
        current,
the water itself, but also the branches and trunks of trees,
and fair-sized boulders that rolled down in the churning water.
        With all
his four legs, he could barely stand there himself, but I learned
to do it, at least for a while, on just these two. He'd watch
150   from the shore, shouting insults and laughing whenever I fell.
I'd pick myself up and do it again and again, till he signaled
I'd lasted long enough. I trained with the Spartan quoit,
flinging the iron circle into the clouds. I practiced
the wrestling holds, and I'd box with the cestus and bared fists—
but that was for relaxation. There were also studies—I practiced
playing the lyre and singing the songs of the gods and giants
and heroes of olden times. He taught me the arts of healing,
which were the leaves and grasses from which to get juices to soothe
one disease or another, or staunch blood, or for sleep.

He showed me which kinds of infections to lance and which do
    better   160
with herbal salves. And then, in the evenings, he used to give lessons
in ethics, theology, law, with discussions of justice and virtue
and the ways of the gods of Olympus, of centaurs on lower
    mountains,
and of men, too. I remember those evenings with gratitude now,
and the fine talk that kept going later and later. I miss that
most of all and believe it was what my mother intended
when she first gave the baby I was into his hands."
The wind was slackening off as the keel ground up on the shore . . .

THE RAPE OF PROSERPINE

CLAUDIUS CLAUDIANUS

Book I

Preface

On what dim dawn did the first clever or reckless soul
   conceive his notion, hew a hull, and fashion
a crude oar to impose on nature and human limit,
   take the water's dare and defy its fickle
moods across the cove, and then, as his courage and skill
   prompted, his heart pounding, further away
from shallows and shore venture off into open water,
   paddling first, then sailing, the winds of the world's
spirit his to master, as he had first mastered his fears
   and the turbulent Aegean's rages and storms   10
he'd somehow survived, riding them out and rounding the point,
   to reach in Ionian shimmer a vista of dreams?

*   *   *

My mind's not right, a jumble of dream-monsters morning
cannot disperse, for huge black horses blot out the sun
as the car of the Queen of Hell comes rumbling by, its shadow
blacker than black to strike terror in mortal hearts.
You, youngsters, stay back! For us who have lived and suffered
to at least the beginnings of wisdom, this is a hard enough trial.
You might not survive who do not know the signs, who have never
seen how a shrine can shudder, its pediments turning liquid,
and an eerie light arising from the sanctum's very threshold

10   to let initiates know how the god we worship and fear
      is at hand. The depths of the earth grind and rumble in menace;
      in the garish light of Eleusis' torches, Triptolemus' vipers
      writhe on the ground, flexing and stretching their argyle necks—
      or may they be Cecrops' snakes his devotees hold holy
      and worship in their weird rites? Out of the murk appears
      Hecate with the eyes of all her three heads blazing
      with knowledge of sky's and earth's and the underworld's close
          secrets.
      Lurching along beside her, tipsy a little as always,
      Iacchus/Bacchus, his temples garlanded (slightly askew)
20   with a crown of ivy. He's wearing a handsome tiger's pelt,
      and holds a ceremonial thyrsus that serves as his cane.
      O gods of the world of shadows, whom ghosts attend, to whom
      mortality owes its all in a debt you wait to foreclose,
      let me see those fields and meadows the Styx surrounds;
      let me hear Phlegethon's murmur and rush and feel the cold
      spray of its rapids and eddies; and confide in me with your stories—
      how with a torch the god of love overcame the god
      of shadows, and tell the tale of his passion for Proserpine,
      the innocent maiden he stole to trouble the land of the living
30   as Ceres, enraged, pursued her lost little girl. That passion,
      that rape, and that long search transformed the lives of mortals
      forever. No longer would acorns and such windfalls suffice us,
      but now, with the secret of grains, and of cultivation, we moved
      out of Dodona's grove and into our sunlit fields,
      away from the beasts and closer, at least a little, to gods.
          Angry, Erebus' lord blazed forth in complaint, to threaten
      war with the gods of the air, if need be, to right this wrong:
      that only he of the deities had no wife at his side,
      none of the comforts and pleasures, none of the satisfactions
40   of divine and even mortal husbands and fathers. No longer
      would he suffer such unfairness, but summoning up the monsters
      and the rest of his hellkite band he rules, and recruiting the Furies,
      he bound them by oath to defy the imperious gods of the light
      and the Thunder-god himself. Tisiphone wields a torch:

in its garish glare, the snakes of her coiffure coil and writhe,
and she summons up the ghosts of heroes to join in his cause.
Earth and water, fire and air are restless as well,
their truce all but forgotten. The titans look up through the new
fissures to see the light of day, and their dreams of revenge
are thoughts. The bloody pirate, Aegaeon clenches his hundred   50
hands to reply to Jupiter's thunderbolt that undid him.
    But it was not fated to happen. The Fates themselves, in fear
for the world they care for, approached him, lowered their heads,
        and implored
with suppliants' streaming tears and touched his knees with their
        hands.
Lachesis first, her hair a crazy tangle, called out
to the lord of night, "Great ruler at whose command we spin,
and who know the ends and beginnings of all things that live and die,
do not undo this work you have given into our keeping.
Do not abandon the sacred treaties you have with your brothers
on which the world's survival depends. Do not make war   60
and loose the impious titans into the air. But go
to your brother Jove and ask. He will grant you that wife
you want and deserve." Pluto's severe expression changed
at the words she spoke. His heart was eased and his anger soothed.
Boreas, nevertheless, was loose, his icy breath
and hail-encrusted wings assaulting the seas and woodlands
in a ruinous frenzy only Aeolus' power could curb,
apprehending and then confining the malefactor.
    Pluto then summons Mercury, Maia's son,
to pass the message skyward to his brother Jove. The wingèd   70
god approaches the dark couch where Pluto reclines.
He reaches for the dust-encrusted and cobwebbed scepter
propped behind his throne. He lifts up his head to speak,
and his words ring out in the gloomy miasma, sound and resound
along the dismal hallways. As far away as the gates,
the belling hound of hell, affrighted, is suddenly mute,
as Cocytus's river of tears, Acheron's turbid flood,
and Phlegethon's fiery current all are abruptly hushed.

Mercury stands there attentive to Pluto's annunciation:

80 "You, sir, alone are free to cross and recross these thresholds
of heaven and hell; I bid you bear to my brother above
my greetings and my complaint, for if his domain is the air
and the earth, I am not without power here below. This darkness
bristles with weapons and strength. Let love, honor, and prudence
speak with a single voice to prompt him to pay me heed!
Let him consider our brother, Neptune, who lolls in the sea
with Amphitrite, his bride. With Juno, our sister, his wife,
Jove finds connubial comfort. We need not allude to the others,
those brief encounters whose issue is nieces and nephews of mine

90 I can hardly reckon. Long life to him and his heirs forever!
But shall I not share in these pleasures? Shall I not also have children
to offer me reverence and love here in the land of shadows?
I cannot accept so unfair or endure so unjust a portion
but must, for the sake of honor, redress this legitimate grievance
at whatever cost—if my words should fall on deaf ears, then
        trumpets
will sound through the chasms of hell to call forth attendant
        monsters
who shall reappear in the light to shroud the face of the sun
in eternal gloom. The world's foundations will be overthrown
for all time and the cosmos itself be wholly undone."

100   Then did the terrible the lord of decomposition fall silent,
and the heavens' messenger, disappearing, returned to the heights
to repeat the defiant words. The lord of Olympus heard him
and considered the difficult question—a wife for Pluto? What
        woman,
noble or common, rich or poor, would consider exchanging
her portion of light and air to preside on that dark throne?
And yet . . . He could see, beyond his brother's demands for justice,
and beyond the not insignificant threats, a fundamental
rightness that he could feel in his bones' marrow—how love
and death reach out to each other in honor and need to sit

110   side by side at the end of each soul's watch, where the efforts
of doing and saying at last are all unsaid and undone.

He thought at once of Ceres, whom men revere at her temple
at Enna. The goddess had prayed for a child and at last had
   conceived
and borne a daughter, and then her womb was exhausted: she knew
this infant, Prosperine, was her first and last and only
child. Any child is dear to a parent, but one like this
is precious beyond all measure. As a cow looks after its darling
wobbly-legged wide-eyed calf, so Ceres tended
her daughter, gazed upon her and watched her grow into girlhood
and ripen to maidenhood. She played as all girls do,
imagined herself a bride, a wife, and a mother . . . but then,   120
in the midst of her innocent play, she would stop in sudden dread
of leaving her mother and home to go and live with some stranger.
In the halls of her mother's palace, suitors from far and wide
assembled: the halls resounded as loud masculine voices
of princes and even gods exchanged their playful banter.
The rival gods who appeared were the valiant Mars and Apollo,
the skillful bowman. The former offered her Rhodope's heights,
and the latter's counter-proposal was the town of Amyclae
and the island of Delos, and also his temple at Claros where Manto's
tears collected to form the miraculous lake. (On Olympus,   130
Mars' and Apollo's mothers, Juno and her old rival
Latona, bickered and argued, each claiming this daughter-in-law
as properly hers.) Ceres couldn't or wouldn't choose,
but recognizing the possible dangers of indecision,
decided to send her daughter somewhere safe—to discourage
any hothead from thinking of kidnapping Proserpine.
(How pathetically blind we are to the plans of the august fates!)
Where should she send the girl for safety? Where can she hide
this jewel of her life? She chooses the loveliest place in the world,
Sicily, that tricorn that sits in the sea like a crown.   140
   It was part of the mainland once, but tides of the raging sea
cut through the neck to leave the channel we now see there.
I can do the geography lesson, point out Palermo, Messina,
and Syracuse, and discourse on the flora and fauna . . . The point
of such set pieces is gaining the reader's confidence, lulling

the suspicious minds of Christians with conventionally didactic,
rhetorical decorations. What Virgil did, and Ovid,
and all those others, I'll do, for it's what the genre requires.
Sicily, Land of Enchantment! (May we have the first slide please?
150 Thank you.) Persuasive descriptions of landscape we've heard before
but, as little children do, we love to have the familiar
repeated, are satisfied to yield our trust to the poet,
so that he may take us farther afield, or below the field
to the gloomy and frightening depths of hell itself. The plains,
the cliffs of the coasts, the rolling hills, and then—slide, please—
the impressive heights of Aetna. Observe that monument
to Jupiter's splendid triumph in the ancient war he waged
against the giants. It is also Enceladus' tomb. His monstrous
body buried below still flexes, twitches, and writhes
160 as he breathes forth in stertorous gasps those sulfurous clouds,
and his spasms of pain and rage still shake the entire island
so that, miles away, in the cities of men, they feel the shudders,
and the walls of their houses tremble, crack, and sometimes fall.
     You can see the volcano's peak, but there's no way to approach it.
The turf, the duff is warm, and then bushes and trees give way
to a no-man's-land of bare and rocky ground, which is warmer,
hot . . . Then steam boils up, and foul-smelling vapors. The
          mountain
quivers beneath your feet and heaves up rocks and boulders
like cinders floating up from a roaring flame. In winter,
170 ice and molten rock contrive to dwell together,
side by side like a husband and wife in a bad marriage.
What's going on? What causes these rents in the earth, these mighty
temblors and noxious smells? Are the winds pent up in the earth's
gut? Is there somewhere below a place where the ocean water
seeps in through some hidden fissure to boil in the mountain's
fire and erupt in these jets of steam? Whatever
the explanation, it's awesome, and the mood of the region is grim.
The brute rage of the place, of nature, and therefore of gods,
no one can question here. Your soles are hot from the wrath
of the very ground that permits from moment to moment your
180   footsteps.

But turn your attention instead to the comfortable plain of Enna,
Ceres' hiding place for her child, unlikely, obscure,
and therefore secure. She bids her good-bye and leaves for Phrygia,
to her mother Cybele's town . . . (Why there? She has to leave,
to go somewhere, so the will of the gods and the fates can work out.
And if some remember Cybele's zealots, the Corybantes
and Galli, and how they howl and dance to a holy frenzy
of self-mutilation that's now forbidden, or think of the ancient
hymn to Ceres we learned in school, and then relearned
when we came at last to Eleusis, it wouldn't be malapropos.)   190
Ceres' amazing pair of wingèd serpents soar
through the upper air and draw her car behind them. Flecks
of venomous foam from their bits dazzle like gems in the sunlight,
and the sun on the golden scales of their necks flashes and glints.
Their heads are crested in emerald green mottled with black
and they rise and swoop like a pair of weird tropical birds,
now high in the air, now low, skimming the ground . . . The wheels
of their vehicle strew the earth's plowed fields with golden grain
that sprouts at once to mark the route of their bounteous journey.
    Behind, in the distance, Sicily dwindles, although in Ceres'
mind it looms as large as ever. She blesses the place,   200
the land where her daughter dwells: that its fields may yield their
        riches
without the promptings of plow or hoe; that the oxen and even
the farmers may gaze on the gifts of their harvests—all her
        harvests—
with wonder and thanks. So the goddess decreed and bestowed.
She turned her face to Mount Ida where her serpents were now
        descending
to land at her mother's shrine, Cybele's court and temple.
    There in a grove of pines that in dead calm quake their boughs,
a holy statue stands, and before it worshippers come
with chantings and sinuous dances. The mountain resounds with
        their cries;
the village of Gargarus trembles; at Ceres' appearance, a sudden   210
hush descends on the throng: the chanters fall silent and drummers
and pipers pause, and the Corybantes sheathe their knives.

Cybele comes to welcome her daughter goddess and bends
her head with the heavily towering crown to honor her guest
and embrace with a ritual double kiss her returning child.
　From his lofty seat in the heavens, Jove looked down and
　　　observed
with heavy heart. His decision was nonetheless made and his
　　　promise
given. He turned to Venus, to let her know what his mind
had resolved, how long ago he had settled on Ceres' daughter,
220　Proserpine, as the spouse of the lord of the underworld.
Thus had they all been bidden by Atropos, that stern
daughter of night who cannot be turned or swayed, and thus
had Themis, the daughter of earth and sky, ratified and proclaimed.
"This is the time," he instructed the goddess of love. "The mother
has left her alone and unguarded. Go down and do your mischief,
summon her out to the meadows at the delicate hour when dawn
has turned the whole world to a pleasantly rumpled bed."
He sighed remembering beds he had rumpled. "Why should
　　　the lord
of the darkness not share in your bounties and blessings? Your
　　　power
extends even there, to the depths of his dismal realm where cold
and unfeeling hearts grow tender and burn from your arrows'
230　　　wounds."
　The goddess departs to do her master's bidding, and with her
Minerva comes, and Diana. The path from heaven to earth
glows from the touch of their feet like the tail of a terrible comet
of evil portent, the kind that sailors despair to behold,
that blood-red trail in the sky, and farmers and villagers fear
to discover the terrible truth of which this sign gives warning
to ships at sea and fortified cities ashore. They arrive
at Ceres' imposing palace with its curtain walls of enormous
240　stones the Cyclopeans hewed and dragged here to pile high
block on block. The gates are iron wrought in the forge,
and the bars on the huge doors and the windows are carbon steel.
In the heart of Aetna, Pyragmon at his forge never made such metal.
Had Steropes' mighty bellows heated his fire so hot,

the stone walls of his hearth would have cracked and molten rock
would have spread in a burning pool on his awesome smithy's floor.
The ceremonial hall of the goddess' palace had walls
covered in ivory panels, and the roof, girdered in bronze,
was supported by massive columns of silver alloyed with gold.

Inside that palace, the daughter Proserpine crooned to herself   250
as she worked at her needlepoint, contriving a welcome-home
gift for her mother's return—and now we describe her design,
inviting the reader to think of Ovid's stitch-by-stitch
account of the work of the great Arachne who vied with the goddess.
Or Virgil's representation of Aeneas' shield, or Homer's
shield of Achilles. The pattern is never far from the poet's
sense of the work he is doing. Proserpine's tapestry showed
how atoms come together; how gods and nature combine
to bring from chaos the ordered cosmos we know and rely on,
the principled scheme of the rising of light and the falling of heavy   260
elements here in the world, the physical laws that govern
the sea and sky and dry land. She tricked out the stars up above
in stitches of gold and silver and suggested the wine-dark sea
with indigos, purples, and violets. You'd have sworn that the water
    moved:
as you stood there and stared at the cloth, you could all but hear
    the boom
of breaking surf on the shingle, and then the intimate hiss
as the water recedes from the beach. She put in the five different
    zones
that Ovid describes and Lucretius—the cold at the poles and the
    torrid
and, in between, the temperate places. How strange is creation,
how rich . . . as the Christians have also remarked in their sacred
    books.   270
This wonder of things we have all known and can surely agree to,
and nobody has an exclusive claim to the wisdom of awe,
for we all look out at the vastness of oceans or up to the skies
at the stars in the heavens. All this she put in her representation
of how things are in the world. She included the nether kingdom
where her uncle ruled over wistful or tormented souls, and her tears

welled up for their sad condition and the fate that waits for us all.
 She was putting in the blue of the ocean's furthest expanses
out toward the edge of the cloth, when guests entered
 unannounced—
280 no mortal women but clearly goddesses. She was afraid
but also impressed with their beauty. Annunciations are painful
honors for those whose lives they interrupt. She blushed
and would have seemed to any impartial observer as lovely
as those divine beings who stood before her, her cheeks
glowing, the gleams of her innocent eyes bright with her youth
and trust. She looked like a picture some artist had made with his
 brushes
and pots of the rarest dyes on a perfect ivory panel.
She had no idea what fate had decided for her, but awaited
as all of us do the unfolding of the plans of implacable gods.
290 The sun was low in the western sky, and the shadows grew longer
over the hills and the plains. In the windows of cottages, lights
flickered on, and then off, as the night came on with its promise
of ease to the labors of men. Pluto had word from his brother
that he should be readied, that this was the night when the promise
 would be
made good. Alecto, whose hair is coifed in a tangle
of vipers, whose breath is rank with the stink of vengeance and
 blood,
had gone to corral the terrible steeds from their murky pastures
on Cocytus' banks where they graze in Erebus' fields and drink
from the fetid pools of Lethe. From their huge lips the flecks
300 of their slobber drug the mind of any creature they touch.
She yoked the two pairs to the chariot-pole of their master's
car: Orphnaeus, the savage; Aethon, the fast one; Nycteus,
the coal-black wonder-horse; and then Alastor, whose blaze
is the mark of Dis himself. They stood in harness and tromped
on the ground with eager hoofs and champed at their bits waiting
for him to take up the reins and crack the whip to signal
the steep ascent of the winding and perilous causeway that leads
from their habitat of shadows to the upper world of light.

Book II

Preface

Orpheus laid down his lyre, as anyone can and, silent,
    was yet himself—but the world was not itself:
the nymphs protested their loss of the pleasure of hearing him sing,
    while rivers mourned in a babble different now,
diminished from what it had been, that nature was sinister, hostile
    with mountains hushed like heifers who think that a lion
lurks behind a nearby tree. Sick at heart, what poet
    can bring himself to believe in the worth of singing?
But something happens. There's news—as there was of Hercules'
    triumph
    over the monstrous horses of Diomedes   10
that fed on human flesh and turned all Thrace to a nightmare
    from which the hero roused it. Orpheus, feeling
a joy no man could help but share, was moved to take up
    his instrument again and touch its strings
to summon forth such chords as harmonize the cosmos.
    The winds and waters were calmed, and flowing rivers
gentled now in their beds. The mountains' daunting stillness
    was happier, eager, as Rhodope's gray boulders
basked in the music they felt like sunshine, and Ossa's snowy
    skullcaps melted in rapture. Poplars, pine trees,   20
and oaks unrooted themselves to attend to the luscious strains
    of the song he improvised. And even Daphne's
laurel, which hated any art form Apollo approved,
    overcame its natural disinclination

and swayed to a music it couldn't resist. Entranced, the fierce
   Molossian dogs forgot their bloodlust and frisked
with emboldened rabbits that once had been their game, while
    lambs
   frolicked and gamboled with wolves, as deer and tigers
and stags and lions performed a queerly pacific quadrille.
30   Orpheus sang of the griefs of heroes who have to contend
with adversarial gods—how Juno had set the tasks,
   ever more demanding, for Hercules
who triumphed, despite her but also because of her, proving his
    greatness
   from the time he had first strangled snakes in his crib
and toyed with their limp but lustrous bodies, scaring his mother:
   "You braved Pasiphaë's bull and took it away;
you tamed the hound of hell; you strangled the Nemean lion
   and trapped the savage boar of Erymanthus.
You mastered the Amazons, loosed their haughty queen's ceinture,
40   and took it home as a trophy; you shot the brazen
birds that harried the crops and the peasants of Stymphalus' lake;
   you killed the three-headed Geryon, stole his herd,
and wrestled Antaeus down—or, better, say, up in the air
   where you choked him at last to death. The hydra's heads
and the wingèd feet of Diana's stag with the golden antlers
   were nothing to you, as Cacus' fiery breath
was nothing. You spilled Busiris' blood and that of the centaurs,
   and bore for a moment the weight of the wide skies
on your broad shoulders . . . " So Orpheus sang, as I
50   sing to you now, Florentinus, whose deeds have roused
my somnolent muse. Grudging and grateful at once, I take up
   my quill yet again and resolve to do my best.

*   *   *

To begin again, to restore, repair, and refresh our exhausted
spirits, the sun reasserts its dazzling self each morning:
down at the quay blue water is spendthrift with gold and silver

benefactions to take away the breath. We gasp
in delight at the dawn's tang and rejoice in being alive.
Proserpine ventured forth . . . Her mother had warned her not to,
but who can oppose what the stern Fates have already decreed?
As she opens the door to go out, its hinges squeak shrill warnings,
to which the volcano rumbles from out of its depths an
    endorsement,
but she seems as deaf as the doorpost. They make a striking tableau: 10
the goddesses Venus, Minerva, Diana, and then herself,
the innocent girl these three connivers are leading astray.
She has no idea what they're thinking. Venus is full of herself
and her headstrong scheme to rule the ruler of ghosts, but she looks
lovely—gorgeous!—her hair in a French knot (bangs in the front,
and a few spit curls at the sides). There's a splendid hairpin her
    husband
Vulcan made at his forge to match the impressive brooch
of amethysts, diamonds, and gold she sports as the clasp of her
    tunic.
Pallas, behind her, is awesome in ceremonial armor
(she is goddess of war, after all), and the helmet she's chosen is
    famous   20
with the carved figure of Typhon, that mutinous giant—baroque,
with his upper body lifeless but the lower limbs still twitching
in rage, pain, or both. That isn't a tree beside her
but the spear she carries, cleverly carved to look like one.
Much less severe is Diana, her hair flowing free and arms
glowing with life and health. Hers is an outdoorsy
look, but the tunic, cut on the bias and artfully draped,
is an apricot crêpe de Chine, just above knee length.
Her bow just now is unstrung, but the arrows are perfectly real
in the elegant quiver she wears on a strap on the left shoulder.   30
If I may, I direct your attention to the sash at her waist—cashmere?
Actually, Pashmina—a silky kind of cashmere
they spin using only the tender chin hairs of certain goats
from particular upland herds. Fit, one might say, for a goddess.
And Ceres' little girl? Elegant, easy, of course,

but notice the cloth of her cape—a specially woven production
she designed herself and commissioned from one of the local
   workrooms,
a tapestry piece depicting the birth of the sun and moon,
Hyperion's children. (He was the son of Heaven and Earth.)
40 Tethys, Hyperion's sister, is holding the two small infants
safe in her bosom. One sees here a cosmological pun
in which one might indulge, but let us content ourselves
with the outward look of the lovely young woman who'd look to be
also a goddess if only she carried some characteristic
emblem—a helmet or quiver and bow. But all she has
is her jasper brooch that fastens her tunic (of peau de soie).
Her mother's pride and joy, who is shortly to be the occasion
of bitterest grief, is walking along on the grass she takes
for granted as safe—as any child ought to be able
50 to do beneath a sky whose gentle blue she never
suspected or thought deceptive. Then comes a troop of naiads,
the opera's supers, but also the representations of rivers,
the Crisinus (or is it perhaps the Crimissus?) and Pantagias . . .
The first is not far from Segesta, the other, a little way north
of Syracuse, where Aeneas once . . . But then who cares?
It's a Hellenistic display of learning, but also a grasping
at proper nouns—the places where holiness once inhered,
and the locals revered or feared, a hoarding away in this capsule
Claudian hopes may endure on its merits (but he will take
60 even space on the shelf in some social-science collection
of ancient place names). The mood of the recitation is grim,
desperate even; the poise is remarkable, nevertheless.
There's Gella, Camerina, and the tallest naiad of all,
Cyane. (How can you have a tall river? The point
is that height is good for the view of parades and also of crimes
and she will report later the dreadful thing she has seen.)
Look at them all as they pass, like Amazons trooping the colors . . .
(That river bears its name because long-haired natives attacked,
whom the Spaniards mistook for women, but that's another story,
70 the point here being the weirdness, wildness, exotic menace

both savage and female—Bacchantic!) The valley exults in the visit,
delights, and its spirit invites Zephyr to come, partake
of the ecstasy here, and suffuse the air with the perfume of
    blossoms,
the loamy smells of the earth still moist with the morning dew,
and the redolence out of the orchards of the first ripening fruits . . .
the smells, one might say, of sex, which is what any valley suggests
to those paying attention. Does Enna conspire with Venus,
or is she merely asserting her monomaniac vision
of what she believes is the deepest truth of things? These same
delicate flavors are those the aged Phoenix gathers   80
to make his miraculous nest of fire from which his rebirth
will define his kind to enlarge what the world must accept as real.
"Come to me," Enna calls out, as a queen to her favorite. "Make me
beautiful, fragrant, new, and worthy to have those dainty
goddesses' fingers plunder my thickets for buds and blossoms."
    Thus she spoke, and Zephyr arose on his gossamer wings
dripping with nectars and attars to asperse the ground like the bed
in a bridal chamber. Wherever he flies, the grass turns brighter,
a slightly more succulent green, and the flowers are all the more
    vivid,
perfect specimens posing for botanical illustrations.   90
Roses are redder, and hyacinths a deeper and richer blue.
Semiramis' famous jewel box couldn't provide
brighter baubles than he broadcasts in his lavish spree,
nor Juno's peacock compete with the breathtaking colors he uses
to adorn the al fresco scene. Heaven's dome is inspired
to answer as well as it can with a new and truer blue.
A fancy, merely? Or is it the way things are at instants
of joy or grief or rage? The landscape engraves itself
upon our souls forever, with the light that way, the colors
daubed with eternity's brushes. This was a scene for the moment,   100
the moment for such a scene, with every hillock and dale
at attention, calling out for attention, appreciation,
and memorization. The streams bubbled up from living rock
clear and cold as truth, and sunbeams sifted through leaves

with the golden sheen of ardor. Trees everywhere stretched forth
their canopies reaching upward, or into the future, the pines
redolent now of the pitch that would see them aboard tall ships.
The smooth cornel flexes eager to turn into shafts
of the sharp spears it may one day become. There is Jupiter's oak,
110   and Apollo's laurel, the sad cypress, the bees' beloved
holm oak where honeycombs brim over, dripping sweetness.
You'd think they'd arranged themselves to hear another cycle
of songs Orpheus might be performing, but all they can see
is women gathering bunches of flowers. In the cool blue
of the lake's glassy surface, their images, inverted,
are picking the topsy-turvy simulacra of posies.
They call to one another, laugh, or hum like birds,
or a swarm of bees criss-crossing the meadow in search of sweetness.
       Venus has urged them . . . But that which a goddess wants to
            suggest
120   seems to arise from one's best and truest self: the blossoms
beckon, blandish, blush in delight as they yield to the hand
for which they seem to know they have always been destined.
       Violets
here, or lilies, or roses, or pretty white privet there,
exult, exclaim, proclaim the moment's perfection, as Venus
stoops for the fragile anemone, her darling Adonis' relic.
Hyacinth's woe, and Narcissus', contribute their profondeurs,
for beauty like theirs never comes without its cost: whatever
is born must die, and what blossoms now must one day droop,
wither, and fade away, leaving behind a mere
130   idea of itself, its wraith, and our sense of diminution.
       Among those lovely creatures gathering loveliness to them,
Proserpine strolls with her elegant osier basket, delighted
at every step and turn at the bounty of colors and smells.
She wreathes some flowers together, twining them into a crown
she sets upon her head . . . Is this at the goddesses' prompting?
Or do they look back and, seeing her innocent gesture, pause,
knowing how she has foreshadowed what fate has arranged, and
       feeling . . . ?

Remorse? Pity at least, for the way things are. The poise
of the gods in the face of what they have seen and must know to
    expect
is a mystery, surely, that mortals can never hope to fathom.   140
Pallas, the goddess of clangor and war has put by her helmet . . .
Or, no, she has woven a halo of flowers about its crown,
turning it tame and attractive, and her sharp spear has become
a pretty pastoral trinket. Call it a portable maypole,
around which the whole world is eager to dance. Diana,
who most of the time is severe as she runs on the mountainsides
with her sleek hounds, has primped at least a little, arranging
sprays of buds and flowers in her hair, a bucolic perfection,
a model out of time for all of time to envy,
but then a roar intervenes, lower than sound but louder   150
than sheer sensation: the earth trembles, and walls of buildings,
forgetting their engineering, quiver, crack, and collapse.
Everyone looks around in some combination of panic
and disbelief, except for Venus, the goddess of Paphus'
enthusiastic cult. She takes this too as her due,
a hymn of praise that the cosmos raises, that now will include
the basso profundo voice of the lord of the dead whose car
is barreling up from his gloomy and airless realm to emerge
somehow into the light. On the way, his enormous wheels
run over Enceladus' huge body, buried below   160
that pleasant island, and crush his monstrous limbs. As he writhes
in sudden pain, the meadows quake and the hillsides quiver.
Saturn's third son careens through caverns and tunnels,
peering in blackness for some faint glimmer of light, some sign
of egress, but nothing, nothing. On all sides there are rocks
on which he pounds in rage and frustration with his huge cudgel.
The entire island shakes with the thunder from underground.
Startled, Vulcan stops at his forge, and his terrified Cyclops
journeymen let their bolts of lightning fall to the floor
to ring on the stone. Lipari and all the Aeolian islands,   170
hearing the dismal resonance, huddle in abject terror,
and far away to the north in the icy Alps one can hear

the echo and re-echo. The Tiber ripples, the Po
sloshes each time the earth shudders in this great labor.
Farther away in the land of Thessaly, Ossa's peak
blows apart from Olympus to make there an instant valley
through which the Peneus flows. (The lake that was there before
shrinks leaving the farmers gifts of new fields to till.)
But in Sicily's hills and mountains, directly above the raging
180   god, is the greatest change, as rocks fly apart and chasms
abruptly yawn as the sounds of hoofbeats and iron-bound wheels
come rumbling forth in crescendo from deep in the bowels of the
        earth.
In amazement and fear, the stars in the sky flee helter-skelter:
the bear that turns on its tail at the pole dives down to hide
in the safety of Ocean's depths; Boötes, the wagoneer,
takes off like a charioteer at a race; Orion, the hunter,
visibly shudders; and Atlas blanches hearing the noise
of those mighty steeds with their breath like smoke and their eyes
        enormous
in the unaccustomed glare of the sun in a brilliant sky.
190   They thrill to the surge of life and the sharp lash on their backs
as Pluto lays on the whip. They hurtle ahead in a blur,
fast as the wind . . . Faster! Like a fleeting thought of a skittish
mind they are there and gone. Their bits are warm with their blood
and they mark their trail in the eddying air with flecks of dazzling
spit and flying droplets of sweat, all deadly poison.
        The nymphs scatter in flight, put to rout. Do any
see the chariot bearing down, the god leaning over
to snatch their companion up in the crook of his arm? Pallas
stands firm, holds up the shield with the blazon of the Gorgon's
200   head, and beside her, Diana strings her bow to prepare
to launch one of her arrows. What can they do to defy
the power of their dark uncle? But how can they stand in silence
to see this outrage? Virgins both, they feel for their friend,
a virgin and therefore a sister. Each of them thinks of herself
in the arms of some ravishing monster, struggling, breathless,
        helpless,

and wishing for death while knowing that worse is about to happen.
Pluto is like some lion that has seized a defenseless heifer
and stands out of reach of the furious cowherds who look with hate
at the shiny gouts of blood on his claws and around his muzzle.
He shakes his enormous mane and yawns in satisfaction   210
and all they can do is shout out impotent imprecations.
    Thus does Minerva defy him: "Lord of the lost, great master
of those whom death has tamed, what madness has driven you out?
Do your unruly subjects revolt? Have the furies turned
their guttering torches to brandish before you? How do you dare
intrude into the realm of your brothers? Return to your proper
place, and find there the wife you are seeking. To share your rule
in darkness, you shouldn't require such beauty or youth." She
        laughed
and raised her shield with its frightening emblem to block the way
of his spirited horses. Before them, the plumes of her helmet waved   220
like fronds of a tropical palm in an onshore breeze, and they shied.
She hefted her ashen spear shaft and braced herself to strike
with its cruel head but the horses, the chariot, too, and the god
glowed with a garish and numinous light from a thunderbolt
Jupiter threw from on high. She froze, as the understanding
suddenly dawned in her mind that Jove had agreed to the union.
Proserpine's father, he signaled consent to the match to which no
lesser god or mortal could now make further objection.
After the flash of light, the crash of the thunder confirmed
the judgment of fate and the gods in an ear-splitting amen.   230
    Minerva stepped aside. Diana too put down
her weapon and called to her friend. If she could not say adieu,
at least she could bid her farewell. "We must yield to greater power.
What our father commands we must all obey, albeit in sorrow,
mourning that you are thus betrayed to darkness and silence,
never more to behold your sisters or play in these fields
of innocence and delight. We who remain here shall weep,
think of you and recall the pleasures we shared together—
for the gods have sundered heaven and earth and so mocked your
        trust;

240 of your child-like faith in the world's benevolence nothing remains,
and the woods will be darker now, the pathways along the cliffs
more fraught with peril, and beasts we chase more savage and fierce.
My moon will not shine so bright, and my brother's fiery son
will be sicklied over; his Delphic shrine will turn thick-tongued . . ."
    There might have been more, but the lord of Hades lashed his
      horses
that hurtled by; the girl in his grip in that flying car
was swept away, her hair flying out behind in the slipstream.
She waved her arms for help, or in protest and lamentation
and cried in vain to the gods in heaven to come to her rescue:
250   "Oh father, save me! Or else send down your thunderbolt
to undo this dreadful thing: obliterate this wrong.
Destroy if you must both crime and victim, but do not leave me,
do not abandon me so. How can a father's love
for a daughter dwindle and dry like a stream in the summer's
      meanness?
What have I done to deserve such anger? Where was my sin?
I look to you for love, or at least for an even-handed
justice, but you desert me, and I am bereft and despair.
Other girls may be seized, carried away and ravished,
but still they are left alive to heal in the light of the sky.
260 I shall be robbed of each of the joys of life on earth
and thrust into darkest Hell, having done nothing, nothing . . . "
Words failed, but her heart and throat kept on with a pure
keening in which the cold winds joined in crazed agreement.
The flowers, she thought, had betrayed her. All those innocuous
      blossoms
the goddess had offered—as bait! She felt a pang of remorse
for not having obeyed her mother who, now it turned out,
was no over-protective parent but properly wary
of bad things that can happen no maiden would ever imagine.
At the thought of her mother she wailed the louder and then called
      out
270 in desperation: "Mother, wherever you are, oh, mother,
hear me, find me, forgive me. Come to me and save me."

But how could she hope her mother could hear, way off at the end
of the earth in those Phrygian mountains where cultists dance in
    their frenzies
and cut their flesh with knives as a sign of divine madness?
    But someone heard her. Closer at hand, stern Pluto was moved
by her fear, her grief, and her beauty. He wiped away her tears
with the hem of his rough cloak and, as well as he could, assured
    her,
"Stop your crying, child. You shall rule with me as queen
of the realm below. I am not after all so bad a husband,
but a son of Saturn, whose order the cosmos obeys, and the brother   280
of mighty Jove and Neptune. You fear my kingdom, I know,
but calm yourself. We too have stars, meadows, and flowers
that never fade but bloom forever and send their delicate
fragrances into the ever-temperate air. I promise
mysterious wonders and simple pleasures. The Champs Elysées
await to delight you, brighten your life, admire, adore you.
I promise that I shall try to make you happy. You leave
the world of the living behind, but all that is mortal will come
at last to present itself to us and bow before us.
You shall be queen of the autumn! A tree, which shall be your tree,   290
produces leaves and branches and fruit of solid gold!
Beneath that tree you shall sit, or better say, preside,
reaping its precious harvest as, barefoot, the kings of the world
march before for you in fear to hear you pronounce your judgments
on the deeds of their just completed lives, and what their rewards
or punishments ought to be. The three fates will be ladies
in waiting attending upon you, and Lethe shall flow to your wish."
    Intrigued? Horrified? Pleased? Most likely, she was struck dumb,
by this bizarrerie, the noise of the horses' hoofs,
and the quiet throng of souls that collected about the cart   300
to welcome their master. Thick as leaves on a hill in autumn
after a wind has passed to shake the boughs, as many
as waves on the sea, or grains of sand in the desert wastes,
the souls of men and women hastened on noiseless feet
for a glimpse of the bride, eager to pay their respects and homage

to Pluto's queen. Their stern master is smiling broadly,
which is most unlike him: they stare from her to him and back,
and are happy but ill at ease, unwilling to trust, or unable,
this unaccustomed mollification. The mighty rivers
that flow through their underground caverns surge and crest in their
310   beds,
as Phlegethon, dripping wet but crackling fire, salutes
with a formal bow his master and mistress and welcomes them
    home.

    The household servants approach to unhitch the team of horses,
take the bits from their mouths, rub them down, curry their coats,
and turn them out to graze in their pastures. Others lug
the cart to the carriage house, while yet others bedeck
the halls, arches, and doorways with tapestries, floral hangings,
and all the appropriate symbols for such an occasion of . . . joy?
What else would one think to call it? The maidens and matrons are
    gathered
320   to serve, to share her delight, to welcome her, to braid
her beautiful hair and then place on her head the traditional veil.
It's a festival, after all, a great occasion—the ghosts
in a moment of rare recreation perform a series of dances,
elaborate graceful figures they weave in the courtyards and halls.
The disembodied wraiths, the Manes, sit down to the banquet
with delicate garlands that wreath their all but substantial brows,
and the usual silence gives way to the faint humming of tunes
recalled from another life—humming, or even singing,
with the various voices harmonizing in rare concord.
330   The darkness and gloom recede, and Minos sets down his urn
of judgment. The rhythmic sounds of blows and the cries of pain
no longer rise up from Tartarus' dungeons, but punishment stops
in a blessed remission no one a moment before could have dreamt of.
Ixion's burning wheel cools and is still. The river
no longer recoils from Tantalus' lips, or the fruit trees' boughs
above his head. Tityus relaxes, looks down, but the vulture,
relenting, no longer claws and gnaws at his quivering vitals.
It flaps its enormous wings and at least for the while is gone.

The furies put by their lists of crimes and take up the wine bowl
to sip, and as they do so, the heads of their serpentine locks   340
dip their delicate tongues to lap what they can. The world
is different, gentled—above, the birds that fly over Avernus'
dismal lake no longer shudder, sicken, and die,
but cross over unharmed. Springs run with milk and honey,
or even wine, and Lachesis—or Atropos her sister?—
has put down the shears that cuts the thread of lives. On earth
nobody dies, no one is killed, neither parent nor child.
Nowhere in all the world does the glare of a funeral pyre
highlight grotesque contortions of grief. Sailors come home
and soldiers return to their sweethearts, every one safe and alive   350
in the countryside and the towns. Charon has no one to ferry
but festoons himself and his skiff and sings like a gondolier.
    The evening star is ablaze and Night in her gorgeous raiment
richly bejeweled is the matron of honor who leads the bride
into the vaulted chamber and touches the nuptial couch
that awaits the pair. She recites the blessings to consecrate
their union and also the dawn of the new age each marriage
ought to portend but this one truly does, a hope
and fresh beginning. The numberless shades have assembled outside
and raise their voices to sing. The palace corridors ring   360
to strains of their stately anthem: "Proserpine, our queen,
and Pluto our lord and master, brother and son-in-law
of Olympian Jove who carries the thunderbolts, you join
two souls intertwined to one in sleep and in waking,
to the end of time and beyond. May your union be rich and fruitful,
with offspring, goddesses, gods, yet to be born, the heirs
of Ceres and Jove that all in Nature in awe awaits."

Book III

Jove summons the gods to a conclave, and Iris departs
at once to deliver his message: the council will meet. That there are
such deliberations, that someone has given thought
to how we live, that our world, whatever its imperfections,
is more than a series of random events, that a kind of intention,
or at least attention, is working, however approximate, vague,
capricious, or even weird it may turn out to be . . . is soothing.
Her subpoena includes the nymphs and river gods, who dry off
and make their way to the chamber of heavenly powers. The lords
of ocean are all in attendance, and the fauns of the woodlands
10   and hills
are milling about in the smallish space reserved for their kind,
alert but apprehensive—they wonder what grave business
has prompted Jove to convene them here together, what threat
impends over the cosmos. The huge room is subdued
and now abruptly silent as the lord of Olympus speaks:
"Our subject today is the sorry state of human affairs
that have troubled me deeply. Saturn's arrangements, well intended
as they may have been, have produced the most unexpected results.
Ease and the life of leisure, my father thought would encourage
20   scholarship, the arts, and refinement of civilization
such that the lives of mortals would resemble our own. Instead,
lethargy, torpor, sloth, and a general trivializing
do neither them nor us any credit. Gods
should not harm or begrudge the good fortune of others
but luxury is no blessing. It dulls the mind and the spirit.

In my father's time, their crops sprang up from untilled fields,
and woodland trees were dripping honey. Mountain springs
flowed clear with water or red with wine that filled men's goblets . . .
and these bounties turned them lazy and stupid. I changed all that
and set them to work, that their wits might sharpen and characters
    shine   30
from abrasions that come with striving, the bearing of burdens, the
    solving
of problems. From victory over adversity, dignity comes,
and honor no gods can bestow. Nature, nevertheless,
complains, questions my judgment, doubts my motives, accuses
my miserliness and harshness. The Mother of all that lives
complains that I make her behave like a stepmother, a stranger
who begrudges her children food to eat. She argues and rails:
'What is the good of a noble soul or a clever brain,
if all that a man can do is run through the woods and gather
acorns to crush and devour—as monkeys would or squirrels?   40
How can you think he'll be happy, cowering there in the bushes,
cold in the wind and rain? What kind of mad scheme is it
that allows him to suffer so to prove he can grow and develop
to realize whatever potential you want him to demonstrate?'
There was no way of shutting her up or changing the subject.
Almost in spite of her nagging, I reconsidered the problem
and had to admit there is something pathetic about how men
are forced to live. There are ways to improve their lot, to let them
fulfil my ambitious plans for what they may one day become.
I have, therefore, decided that Ceres will teach them farming   50
and let them know her secrets of sowing and reaping grain.
She has no idea what has happened to her daughter, Proserpine,
but she roams the earth in the hope that she may yet find her child,
safe and sound. It's sad. I swear, nevertheless,
should any god presume to tell her what happened, reveal
how the girl has been snatched away, or hint that my brother Pluto
did this thing, that god shall feel my implacable wrath
and the blows of my thunderbolts—and then he or she will face
a new and sterner lord in my brother and son-in-law,

60 Pluto, who will be angry—as will all his fiercely loyal
    (and loyally fierce) wardens of his dungeons and torture chambers
    that are worse than our worst nightmares. Such," said the
        mighty god,
    "is my judgment and will. Let the fates, implacable and unswerving,
    see it be done," and gravely Jupiter nodded his head.
        Far away in a sacred cave, where the Corybantes'
    knives and other such grim paraphernalia hung
    high on the walls, a restless Ceres tossed in her bed,
    afflicted by terrible dreams of unclear but ominous portent.
    A confused and confusing scene: a house, but a bare ash tree
70 is growing up in the courtyard . . . Or does it have buds and leaves?
    Or is it, perhaps a laurel, the symbol of maidenly virtue
    ever since Daphne's time, and why is it fallen, destroyed
    by the furies of hell? She is running, or trying to run, but her steps
    are labored and slow, and her long black robes are a burdensome
        tangle.
    Why is she wearing black? Is she in mourning? For whom?
    (For whom else could it be?) She wakes in a panic. Her daughter
    appears before her eyes. In another dream? A waking
    vision? The girl is shut up in a dungeon, bound in chains . . .
    She tries to persuade herself that her daughter is safe, is enjoying
80 the sunlit and flower-bestrewn meadows on Aetna's flanks.
    But not in the vision or dream. She is ashen pale, and her hair
    hangs down in lank disarray. Her eyes are as dull and blank
    as those of a corpse. The mother's heart is wrung. She would call
    but cannot form the words. Only with terrible effort
    can she manage at last to cry out, as if across a chasm,
    "Is that you, darling? Where are you? Who has done this? Why . . . ?"
    It was indeed her daughter, calling back, in sorrow,
    in pain that accused the wretched mother, "How can you dance
    in religious rites when your child is suffering so? A tiger
90 comes to the aid of its cub. See how I suffer, shut up
    in this distant, dismal cavern, your Proserpine, who loves you
    and looks to you for rescue." There was more, but words gave way
    to the infant wail that Ceres remembered from years before

when the baby girl had first called out for food, for warmth
and protection. How could she not respond? She held out her arms
in a vain attempt to reach her daughter, who tried to grasp
the proffered hands, but her cruel fetters held her fast,
clanking a grim tattoo as they rattled across the stones—
the worst noise Ceres had ever heard, and it woke her
in a cold sweat, but the terror remained, and the pity. A dream?   100
But not necessarily only a dream: something behind it
was true, was real! Is her daughter safe . . . ? She remembers the ache
of empty, extended arms and feels the need to embrace
her child once more. She was wrong to have left her alone. That
      island
is no guarantee of safety. A more obscure retreat,
that's what she ought to have thought of. She runs to her own
      mother,
Cybele, to explain her sudden panic, her guilt,
and need to attend to the dream's warning. The elder goddess,
sympathetic, listens to Ceres' not quite coherent
list of evil omens, unlucky signs and portents   110
besides the dream: how a crown of corn sheaves slipped from
      her head;
how suddenly tears have welled up for no good reason; how flutes
whenever she played them have sounded the minor modes of dirges;
and how drums and cymbals she touched with her fingers and palms
      have echoed
the rhythms of funeral marches. Her mother is reassuring
and suggests that Jove would never abandon his own daughter
or leave her unprotected. His thunderbolts are awesome,
and what temerarious person or god would think to defy
the lord of Olympus? A sensible thought . . . but irrelevant, useless,
as both of them know, and the mother bids her daughter farewell,   120
hoping that all will be well, and that she may return forthwith
to report that her nervous fancies were groundless and quite absurd.
      Ceres thanks her and mounts her dragon-driven car,
but not even dragons are fast as her thoughts; her fears and desires
are already there, and she peers ahead for Sicily's coastline

(Mount Ida, behind her, is not even out of her sight). She lashes
her magical beasts and they flap their huge, iridescent wings.
She flies, as one says, like a bird—but a bird that has built its nest
on a delicate sapling—an ash, let us say—and it worries, imagines
what a wind might have done to the tree, the nest, and the tiny
130   nestlings,
or what rude boy, or cat, or snake might have found her darlings,
and she flutters her wings as fast as her straining heart is beating.
So does Ceres hurry, frightened, reproaching herself,
and trying not yet to abandon hope—lest that somehow invite
the bad fortune she dreads. There, below, she espies
the island, the castle walls . . . But the gate is ajar, the courtyard
deserted, the doors wide open. Inside, the hallways are empty.
Where are the guards? The servants? She tears from her head the
      wreath
of grain and shudders and moans. She rends her clothing. She cannot
140   speak or even breathe, but staggers from room to room:
each doorway's empty vista assaults, reproaches, accuses,
condemns . . . She remembers her dream and the arduous effort of
      every
step she took, and takes. She feels it again in her calves
and ankles. She reaches her daughter's bedroom. The little loom
on which the girl had been working waits in the corner, the weaving
a terrible thing to behold left off that way. But worse,
Ceres sees above it the web of a spider, the only
sign in the desolate room of weaving, work, or life.
Its fragile weight is too much: she draws a painful breath,
150   but will not weep. She will not. She kisses the frame of the loom
her daughter's hand had touched. She touches the delicate threads
as if they were strands of her daughter's beautiful hair. The spindle
she recently used hangs down like a dead thing. Ceres sits,
or in fact collapses, upon her daughter's now empty bed,
touches the pillow that often touched the young girl's cheeks,
and strokes it as if it were flesh. She is not mad but wishes
madness might come to bring her relief, as it can for the desperate.
She looks about at the playthings, pictures, clothing, bereft . . .

They would, if they only had souls, share her perfection of grief.
She is like the astonished shepherd or cowherd who counts his flock   160
and realizes some are missing, that predators must have attacked,
and he calls out to the empty air while he searches the hills
for whatever the lion has left in the scrub of the mauled carcass.
Distracted, dazed, she wanders from one room to the next
until, at last, she discovers a living being—Electra,
one of the old sea nymphs and Proserpine's nurse. She lay
on the floor, disheveled, undone with grief, lamenting the loss
of the girl she had loved, cared for as her own, and used to dandle,
feed, caress, protect . . . One tries one's best, but fate
is lurking, crouches, waiting to pounce, and one's love and care   170
are a nullity, as one's being, one's whole life is destroyed.
Her clothing is fouled; her face, tear-streaked, is blotched with dirt;
her rolling eyes are blank; and she moans. Has she gone quite mad?
Ceres approaches and asks what terrible thing has happened.
Electra stares for a moment, unresponsive, then bawls
as if in the first cruel moment. Ceres offers her comfort,
the frayed shreds of the hope she is keeping alive in her own
heart: "Does Jove no longer rule in the heavens? What reckless
creature would raise a hand against his daughter? Have titans
and giants overthrown the cosmic order? Is Typhon   180
back, or has Aetna vomited up from its fiery depths
Enceladus for another useless and doomed assault?"
None of this seems to be getting through to Electra. Ceres
tries another tack. "Tell me, where are the servants?
Where are the guards? The companions? Where has Proserpine gone?
Speak, woman! When did you see her last? And where?"
But still nothing. She seizes her, holds her tight by the shoulders,
and shakes her. The eyes stop rolling, and the nurse shudders in
        shame
and sorrow mixed together, as bitter as bile and gall.
She wishes she were dead, so as not to have to face   190
the mother now and tell the tale, but Ceres' grip
is unrelenting. At last Electra speaks: "Giants
would have been better. Those brutes we understand, their ungainly

passions, their childlike hungers and lusts. It's the wounds of gods
we should fear, for they have a plan and purpose—to crush the spirit,
undo us, and turn us to abject slaves who perforce accede
to wrongs on every side. What you see here is Heaven's doing!
  "The house was just as you left it, quiet, secure. The girl
would never have thought to venture across the threshold to
    meadows
200 even in sight of the gate. What you commanded, she did,
remaining inside at her loom, enjoying the sirens' songs,
and never complaining. We talked, played games . . . " She took a
    breath
to calm herself and then continued. "Until the goddess
appeared. Or three of them, Venus, with Diana along, and Minerva,
all come to visit their lonely sister! How did they know
she was here? I never thought to wonder, but only later
could see it must have been planned. But I can't think what I'd have
    done,
I had guessed. Venus? Diana? Minerva? Together?
I am a mere sea nymph! And they were all smiles and kisses,
210 and I never thought to suspect them. They wanted to cheer her up,
to entertain her, to make her feel like a sister, a goddess,
who shouldn't be rusticated by a mother more fond and foolish
than most mothers are—meaning you. They said it and laughed,
and poor Proserpine joined in, assuming good will, good faith . . .
How is a child to know what the wicked world has prepared?
She ordered a feast with elegant dainties and nectar the gods
and goddesses like. They ate, drank, and had fun . . . Diana
let the girl try on a hunting costume. Minerva
lent her the splendid helmet she wears with the horsehair plumes.
220 Giggling children, they were. And Venus proposed they go out
to gather flowers. It wasn't out of the blue: they'd been talking
of how, in Sicily, flowers bloom all year, how the winters
can still provide bouquets to dress up a room or persuade
a beautiful girl to listen to a gallant's stories and songs.
Proserpine had explained how this happens here in the South,
and Venus responded quickly, as if to our darling's suggestion.

Proserpine thought, I am sure, of what you had told her. But now
how could she not go along without seeming rude and suspicious?
I was uneasy by then and let her know. I begged her
not to go out, to obey her mother, to do as she'd promised . . .   230
But how could she listen to me, her silly old nurse, when her sisters,
goddesses after all, were proposing a walk in fields
she'd played in before and known for years? Her pride was involved,
and the more I implored the more she was fixed in her purpose. She
        told me
she'd never be out of sight of these sisters, friends, and protectors,
and all the nymphs would come. There is surely safety in numbers.
No point, then, in going on. Then or now. She'd decided,
and out they went to the hills to see how the grass is green
all year long and flowers bloom the entire winter.
    "Dawn, it was, and the grass was still bejeweled with dew.   240
The violets looked to be candied. The sun climbed high in the sky—
but then instead of the glare of noon it was suddenly dark,
ghostly and leached of color. One's blood froze, and the earth
rumbled and shuddered with wheels grinding and hoofbeats
        pounding,
as the juggernaut bore down on the meadow. The girls scattered,
shrieking to one another in fear of this nuncio
of death—or was it Death himself? The rivers froze
in their beds and the grass withered and died wherever the hoofs
had touched it. The flowers shriveled: roses and lilies turned
black and their sickened petals crumbled apart. The flecks   250
of foam from the horses' bits were a deadly defoliant spray . . .
But then they were gone, moved on or returned to where they'd
        come from,
and she was gone. Those goddesses, too, disappeared, having done
what it was they had come to do. We searched, we did what we
        could . . .
Cyane, dazed, grief-stricken, we found—the wreaths she had braided
about her head were now funereal black. We asked her
what had become of our darling? Her only reply was to weep
uncontrollable tears. We asked her who drove the car.

Had she managed to see his face? Could she describe him? She
    moaned,
260   cried, and dissolved into tears—not in a manner of speaking
but literally, as her legs and arms disappeared and her body
flowed into water, murky at first, and then crystal clear.
The sirens took wing and flew to the coast where they are still
    singing,
but their songs are now designed to mislead ships, for they hate
men who do such things and would punish at random whoever
may hear their seductive strains. They lure them to sudden
    destruction.
And I, alone am left," Electra said, "to mourn
in these empty rooms the enormous loss that fills their spaces."
    It also fills Ceres' soul. Her mind gags: it cannot
270   accept that this has happened. She raises her eyes to heaven
and rages against the sky with the low groans a tigress
might make in grief and anger in the distant forests of Persia
after a huntsman has kidnaped her cubs to tame for the Shah's
entertainment . . . She rumbles in pain and outrage and follows
the huntsman's trail, ready to pounce, claw, maul him,
to free her babies . . . But he has prepared a mirror to dazzle,
confuse, and at last undo her. She sees in its convex surface
her own reflection, but smaller. She picks it up—the mirror—
and, taking it for her cub, carries it back to her lair.
280   In such pathetic distraction, the mother wanders and rages,
defying the other gods of Olympus: "Give her back!
Ceres commands it. Who do you think I am? No common
dryad, not one of those rabble of nymphs, but the daughter Cybele
bore to Jupiter's father, Saturn. What insolence is this?
A mistake? It must be corrected, reconsidered, undone . . .
What is the point of lineage? What is the good of virtue,
if it be rewarded thus? Venus, traitor, tramp,
how can you show your face in heaven or earth? My daughter,
a virgin, had nothing to do with you! An innocent child . . .
290   And you, Pallas, and you, Diana, aides and abettors,
were accomplices in this dirty business? Panderers! Pimps!

The towel girls of a bagnio! What kind of goddesses are you?
Scythian savages' barbarous totems, spattered with blood,
would never behave so badly, tolerate such injustice . . . "
She continues for some time these pathetic ravings. The gods'
and goddesses' hearts are wrung; they are shamed to hear her
        complaint,
but are sworn to silence. Their only answer is tears that spill
from their eyes to their downturned faces. She subsides, as her anger
changes to something even more bitter, a wretched despair.
She begs not for the daughter to be restored but only   300
to know the truth, to be rid of the agonizing hopes
that still torment her, disaster's other pincer. "Justice,
never mind. " she says. "It is fate, blind and indifferent.
Nothing we ever do deserves the good or the bad
that randomly befalls us. But grant me the comfort of knowing
whatever it was, however dreadful. Who did this thing?
Who was that chariot's driver? Latona, to you I appeal,
mother to mother. My only child has been taken away . . .
Show me that compassion I'd have for you, if Apollo
and Diana both disappeared and you were the one here,
        weeping . . . "   310
    Nothing! Not a whisper. "You all desert me?" she asks.
"All heaven is joined against me?" And having asked that question,
she suddenly understands that they are combined or enjoined,
but somehow or other allied, and her anger returns in a rush.
She defies them all: "Why bother? Why do I waste my breath?"
She feels the strength of her new resolution, a reckless defiance.
"Is it war with the gods? Very well! Damn you all! I will search
to the ends of the earth to find her, will scour the hidden places
from the furthest shores of the Red Sea to the frozen Alpine crags.
I will ignore extremes of heat and cold, and pursue   320
day and night through dust and mud in cities and towns,
meadows, deserts, and forests, while you look down and laugh
in scorn . . . But I will succeed. I swear that I shall find her
if it takes me the rest of eternity. Ceres is not yet vanquished!"
    Thus she spoke and flew at once to Aetna's familiar

slopes to fashion herself the torch she'd need in her quest.
Near Acis' stream is a wood, where the sad Galatea comes
to soothe her troubled spirit. Its dense thickets enclose
a sacred glade where the trees are hung with Jupiter's trophies,
330   fruits, as it were, of his labors: shields, huge swords, the heads
and bodies of slaughtered giants and dismembered monsters.
       Serpents'
shed skins festoon the branches like crêpe paper catenaries
at a ghoulish masquerade. On one tree, heavily laden
by the weight of the metal, the naked swords of the hundred-
       handed
Aegaeon rustle like wind chimes. Nearby, are Coeus' arms
and Mimas' spoils, and the booty Jove took from Ophion dangles
not far away. On the tallest tree, a pitch-pole pine,
the king of the giants, Enceladus' armor is out on display
and would long ago have bowed the huge trunk to the ground
340   were it not for an oak against which it leans for support. This grove
is sacred: not even the Cyclops ventures there, but Ceres
is undeterred. Its sanctity only serves to provoke her,
inflaming her passion. Her will is fixed as is all her devotion.
She has come with a fine-honed axe resolved to hack from these
ancient, sacrosanct trees the brand she requires. The glaring
outrage of the deed will help dispel the darkness
into which she is eager to thrust and plunge, as if with a knife
in the heart of whoever it was who stole her beloved child.
She strolls from tree to tree, like a connoisseur of timber,
a dealer in lumber for builders and cabinet-makers, a sawyer,
or a shipwright, say, who is thinking that this might be good for a
350   mast,
or that for a watertight keel. She touches the bark and feels
the strength of the grain of one, and the next, and then walks
       further
to see what else is on offer. She has in her mind that enormous
flambeau with which she will hunt for some trace of her daughter,
a huge tree it would be with its rich ramifications
that will make a fire that burns the brighter . . . And then she sees

the perfect specimens, two of them, cypresses, side by side,
tall and their canopies both immense. Such trees she has never
before beheld in all her extensive travels. These
are the very ones she wants. She strikes at the first with her axe,   360
and then the other—deeper, greedier cuts than any
lumberjack would attempt, because of her rage, her pain,
her need to exert herself, to do . . . something. Her hair
streams in the wind and her gown flies out behind her to make
a bizarre tableau of . . . What? Determination? Distress?
Utter madness? All the above? Her strenuous blows
ring out in the gloom as if she were striking a tocsin. The trees
shudder and fall together, as they had flourished and grown
together, and raise a cloud of dust from the trembling earth.
For miles around wood nymphs cry out in terror, and fauns   370
weep at the devastation, the terrible desecration.
But Ceres does not pause even an instant. She seizes
the trees and raises them high above her head. She lopes
upward, ascending the slope of Aetna right to the lip
of the hot caldera. The vegetation gives way to an empty
plain of lava, cooled to black irregular shapes.
Here and there are cracks and fissures, some of them sporting
plumes of steam in which the acrid vapors mix
for which the volcano is famous. The ground underfoot is warm,
hot, but she keeps on going, approaches the edge of the crater,   380
and thrusts the cypresses down into the mountain's maw.
Imagine ghastly Megaera, Acheron's daughter and Night's,
with the yew-tree torch she brandishes high to light her way
to the walls of Cadmus' city or perhaps to Mycenae's hill,
and think how the shadows leap grotesquely and dance in menace.
That was the picture Ceres had in her mind, and she felt
the intense heat from the mouth of the furnace into which
she had thrust her trees. They blocked the opening, stopped up the
          smoke
and flames, and the mountain shuddered and groaned from the
          pent-up pressure.
As descant to the basso profundo rumble, a crackling   390

noise begins to sound—the cypress branches are blazing,
having been set alight by the hot sulfurous vapors.
Ceres waves them about in the air to make them burn
hotter, ever more brightly, and to keep them from being consumed,
she sprinkles on them the magic powder Apollo uses
to protect his horses and keep his chariot safe from the sun's
incinerating heat, and his sister Diana, too,
dusts her team of oxen that draws the moon through the sky.
　　Night has fallen now and the world is preparing for sleep,
400　but Ceres can no longer imagine such things. Her blood
boils, burns, the wound in her soul is hot and fresh,
and the trees she holds above her head turn everything lurid,
as she sets out on her journey, moaning aloud, addressing
her daughter—but knowing perfectly well that no one can hear:
"These are not the torches I dreamt I would one day carry.
I had thought—as every mother does—of the wedding torch
I'd hold to light your way from a happy nuptial feast
to the bridal chamber and bed and the start of a decent life.
Look at me now! A garish vision of rage and woe,
410　with distorted shadows I cast behind me of how the fates
can sport even with gods, turning the commonplace
into a sudden horror. What men must feel, I feel—
puzzled and hurt that my brief moments of peace and contentment
should have so piqued their envy, or invited such brutal redress.
Those peasant women who never smile, lest the gods impose
a tax on their minuscule pleasures, are right after all. I admitted
my joy and pride in my daughter, my only child, but enough
to satisfy whatever maternal dreams I'd had.
With you, I was truly content, the equal even of Juno;
420　now I am less than the least human beggar or outcast.
My case is worse, for mortals' suffering sooner or later
comes to an end, but mine will go on and on, forever.
I rage against Jupiter's will, but still a part of me knows
it wasn't his doing but mine, my own mistake, my folly
leaving you here while I was gallivanting elsewhere,
in the train of the mother goddess. I knew there was danger: I took

precautions, but not enough. I should never have gone in the first
    place.
It's me the fates want to punish: they are only using you,
knowing how much the worse your pains are for me to endure.
    "Where have you gone, my baby? Where are you hidden? In what   430
part of the earth or sky or sea cave? Where shall I look?
Someone must help me, pity me, or pity you, who have done
nothing, nothing at all! But I shall do what it takes
to find some trace, some clue, some faint hoofprint or rut
of those wheels, a bent grass blade, a broken twig. I will comb
the terrain, with unflagging persistence, and, sooner or later,
    discover
some hint of who it was, god, demigod or mortal,
and hate shall bear me up, for I shall imagine . . . HER!
Dione, Venus' mother, reduced to this sorry condition.
She deserves this, not me. And the day will arrive when my labors   440
succeed, or luck, or a dream that will speak to me and give me
my beautiful daughter, happy and healthy, once more in my arms."
    She sets off through the meadow she hates now, her torch aloft.
Tears pour down from her eyes into the wagon-wheel ruts
as she follows, step by step, to the shore where her flambeau's glare
shines on the black water in garish, erratic flickers
of dubious portent up and down the coast. The dogs
in Scylla's distant cave are roused from their drowse: their baleful
baying into the darkness resounds on obdurate cliffs . . . .

                        *   *   *

[It breaks off here. A reversal in Florentinus' fortunes?
Or Stilicho's? Or Claudian's? Surely of Rome's. The Christians
have come, and the Huns approach. That baying, that eerie gloom
broken by random flashes will stretch out a thousand years.]

Afterword

David Konstan

STATIUS WROTE IN LATIN TOWARD THE END of the first century A.D., Claudian at the end of the fourth. By this time, Greek mythology was already ancient and had long been more or less naturalized in Italy, thanks to the prestige of Greek culture and the fascination of the myths themselves. The story of Achilles, which Statius began to recount in Latin hexameters, had, of course, hoary epic credentials, going back to Homer's *Iliad*, which had been composed nearly a millennium earlier. Claudian's theme, the rape of Proserpine, was known in a version almost as old: the second "Homeric Hymn," so called because it too is composed in the formulaic diction that characterizes the Homeric epics. Numerous other texts repeated, amplified, varied, or alluded to the myths or legends concerning Achilles and Proserpine before Statius and Claudian chose to retell them yet again. Some of these renditions have survived; many others have been lost and are known to us only through brief fragments and later references, if they are known at all. But the ancient readers of Statius and Claudian were acquainted with at least the major versions, and could be counted on to recognize and enjoy the novel ways the poets had handled them.

Some of the special effects Statius and Claudian achieved depend on relatively obscure details in the traditional accounts, to which the poets refer obliquely. To take but a single example: at verses 88–89 of book 1 of Statius' *Achilleid* (references are to the translation), Neptune reassures Thetis, the ocean nymph who is mother to Achilles:

"Peleus' son shall shine like the child of Jove you wanted, doing his father proud." Now a sophisticated reader in antiquity would have recognized here an allusion to the story that Jupiter had wanted to father a child on Thetis, but desisted because of an oracle that said Thetis' son would be stronger than his father; indeed, Statius mentions Jupiter's qualms on this score in the opening verses of the poem. As a result, Jupiter bestowed Thetis upon Peleus, and their son proved to be the most powerful of all the warriors at Troy. In fact, Statius went further in helping the reader to catch the reference. Translated literally, the Latin text reads (1.90): "Stop complaining about Peleus and a low-class marriage—you'll think you bore Achilles to Jove," as though Thetis were still smarting, as some earlier versions supposed, at having been forced to wed a mortal, which Statius, with a typically Roman aristocratic sensibility, renders in terms of marrying beneath one's station. David Slavitt, in his translation, omits the mention of Thetis' complaints—wisely, in my judgment: modern readers may not have so thorough a knowledge of the mythological background, and in that case subtle in-jokes may leave them wondering what they have missed, rather than going with the flow of the poetry. Slavitt's version conveys the essential point: that Achilles will be every bit as good as Jupiter's own son. If you have caught the overtone as well and realize that Achilles all but was the son of Jove, so much the better.

Subtleties such as these invite footnotes and commentary, which are death to poetry, as T. S. Eliot belatedly perceived when he regretted having supplied them for his poem, *The Waste Land*. Slavitt's vibrant translations let the poems speak for themselves, unencumbered by a learned apparatus. What is more, they work, because the heart of Statius' ironic sensibility does not depend on such pedantries. Statius's decision to begin his epic about Achilles with the episode of his disguise as a girl, in an attempt at draft evasion on the eve of the Trojan War, contrasts so startlingly with the image of the fierce warrior we know from Homer's *Iliad* that any reader who has heard the name Achilles is bound to notice that Statius is up to something different. It is as though Statius were deliberately flying in the face of Horace's advice to poets in his *Art of Poetry* (120–22): "If by any chance you *should* redo Achilles, make him restless, irascible, pitiless, bitter, insisting that laws were not made for him and claiming everything by force of arms" (cf. Rosati 1994: 5–6; King 1987: 130–33).

Homer alludes in passing to a connection between Achilles and the island of Scyros (one tradition had it that Achilles fathered a son, Neoptolemus, on the local king's daughter on the occasion of a raid on Scyros), but he does not so much as hint at an incident involving transvestism. For that matter, the entire *Iliad* contains hardly a mention of the centaur Chiron and his role as tutor to Achilles in the skills and courtesies of war (at l. 157 it is said in passing that Achilles learned medicine from Chrion; cf. Roussel 1991: 100–103). To be sure, Achilles' youth was not Homer's theme. The *Iliad* tells the story of a crisis that develops within the Greek army in the tenth and final year of the war at Troy, when Achilles, insulted by Agamemnon, withdraws from the fighting, with the result that the Trojans nearly destroy the Greek fleet. Achilles returns to battle only after his dearest friend is slain by the enemy. Achilles' childhood is extraneous to this narrative, and Homer largely ignores it, just as he ignores the legend about Zeus' fear of marrying Thetis and the prediction that Thetis' son would be stronger than his father. Indeed, Homer disregards even the famous judgment of Paris, which was the cause of the Trojan War itself. For all its bulk, the *Iliad* is a highly focused work of art, and anything not immediately relevant to the quarrel between Achilles and Agamemnon is secondary and may be elided.

But the differences between Homer's and Statius's treatment of Achilles are clearly due to more than a shift in the time frame of the story. For example, Homer did not simply overlook Chiron: rather, he deliberately suppressed his role and substituted for the centaur an old retainer named Phoenix, who reared the boy from infancy; many a time, he says, he had to change his soiled tunic when the baby hero spit up his food (*Iliad* 9.488–91). Homer seems also to have known, and rejected, the tradition according to which Jupiter married Thetis off to Peleus, Achilles' mortal father, for fear that the child would be stronger than his begetter. When Achilles suggests to Thetis that she ask Jupiter to favor the Trojans so that the Greeks may repent of their slight to him, he recommends that she remind Jupiter of the time when the other Olympian gods rebelled against him, and he triumphed thanks only to Thetis' initiative in summoning the hundred-armed Aegaeon to assist him—Aegaeon, who, Achilles casually remarks, is stronger than his father (1.393–406; cf. *Achilleid* 1.208–10). It is plausible to see here a sidelong allusion to the legend of Achilles' own parentage (see Ballabriga 1996). Once again it appears that Homer was not oblivious of the traditions Statius follows, nor did they simply lie outside the scope of his plot; rather, Homer adapted the mythic materials at his disposal to a particular conception of his hero, and omitted what seemed contrary or irrelevant to his theme.

Though Statius obviously chose to widen the range of his epic to include a great deal more of Achilles' life than Homer had, he too eschewed the temptation to present a complete biography. Thus, like Homer, Statius elected to skip over the narrative of Achilles' ancestry and birth, save for a few cursory references to Jupiter's role like the ones we have noted, and to begin his epic with the hero's adolescence and his mother's anxious efforts to keep him out of the coming war. As it happens, Statius, for whatever reason, broke off his incipient epic at the point when Achilles' disguise is penetrated and he joins the campaign, though in the proem Statius had promised to carry the account through to the hero's death at Troy (it is possible that Statius died while at work on the poem). The fragmentary treatment has its own effect: the image of Achilles dodging the draft in drag dominates the epic, and limns a figure palpably different from Homer's tragic warrior.

Statius did not invent the episode of Achilles' disguise as a girl on Scyros (for the nymph, see Roussel 1991: 123–41). It is recorded as a well-known part of Achilles' history by the systematic mythographer Apollodorus (*Library*, 3.174), who may have been more or less contemporary with Statius, and there are references to it in earlier Greek poetry, for example the idyll attributed to the pastoral poet Bion (2.5–9) and dating to the second century B.C. It is possible that the episode was mentioned in ancient epics, now lost to us, which treated the events of the Trojan War in various ways; marginal notes on the *Iliad* deriving ultimately from scholars working in Alexandria in the third century B.C. (the D scholia to *Iliad* 19.326) suggest that the events on Scyros were treated in more detail in some of these poems. It may be doubted, however, that Achilles' transvestism had ever been developed at any length in epic poetry before: the conventions of archaic epic, and even of more sophisticated and bourgeois compositions like the *Argonautica* of Apollonius of Rhodes (third century B.C.), were too elevated to dwell on so undignified a theme (cf. Dilke 1954: 10–12).

Both Sophocles and Euripides wrote tragedies with the title *Scyrians*, but Sophocles' version, at least, may have dramatized the fetching to Troy of Neoptolemus, Achilles' son by Lycomedes' daughter, rather than the business of Achilles' masquerade (so Radt 1977: 418 on Sophocles; on Euripides, cf. Roussel 1991: 130). The story seems to have been illustrated in a fifth-century B.C. painting by Polygnotus (Pausanias 1.22.6), and the topic was certainly a favorite with the Roman wall-painters who decorated the luxury mansions at Pompeii and elsewhere (see *LIMC* 1.55–69; cf. Ovid, *Art of Love* 1.687–704). Villas such as these are, indeed, just the sort that Statius himself dearly loved and celebrated in his occasional verse, *The Silvae*.

The tale of Achilles' disguise has the appearance of a myth of maturation from the status of preadolescence when a boy still dwelt among the women of the house, to adulthood, when he would be expected to manifest an interest in manly occupations such as warfare, and also in women both as objects of sexual desire and as potential bearers of his offspring. Achilles' assumption of the guise of a girl may be seen, on this interpretation, as an allegorical expression of the still equivocal sexuality of the child, at the same time that it locates the adolescent in the liminal space characteristic of rites of passage, in which normal codes of dress and comportment are typically suspended or inverted for a while (see Turner 1969; Rosati 1994: 11–19). Statius himself is sensitive to this symbolic dimension of the episode on Scyros, but it is not the aspect that he emphasizes. Rather, he delights in the naughty humor of the situation and the deflation of epic pretentiousness. The effect is to import a gentle irony and humor into a war story that bristles with patriotic fervor and bloodlust.

For Statius, even in this epic account of youthful valor, remains the poet of the *Silvae*, that collection of poems written largely for patrons, in which he celebrates the tranquil luxury of prominent Roman aristocrats, safely ensconced in their private villas, away from the turmoil of politics and war, and dedicated—some of them—to an Epicurean serenity that is at the opposite pole to the military values memorialized in the Homeric *Iliad*. Statius writes of one friend's estate (1.3.34–37, 47–49, 90–94):

What shall I sing first, what next, where cease in silence? Shall I admire the gilded beams or the citrus-wood posts or the marble glowing with its stenciled veinwork, or the nymph-statues scattered through the rooms . . . ? I saw works of art and ancient handiwork in metal come alive in every form—it would cost me to recall the figures in gold, the ivory, and the jewels worthy of gracing fingers. . . . Here it is that those men of character ponder weighty matters, here are contained in tranquil brow fecund repose, sober virtue, hale splendor, and dalliance without indulgence such as old Epicurus himself would have preferred, leaving Athens behind and his garden deserted.

It is in vacation homes such as these, where lavish elegance coexisted with the cultivation of taste and philosophy, that Statius could have enjoyed the light-hearted renditions of Achilles in girl's attire on the island of Scyros that were so popular with the villa crowd; perhaps he also contemplated the possibility of reciting his aborted epic in such surroundings (cf. 1.3.102).

Consider Thetis' words when she first becomes aware of Paris' abduction of Helen: "Was it for this that I sent him [Achilles] away to Chiron's cave, to safe obscurity there? And what did he learn but to carry deadly weapons and rough-house, as the centaurs did with the Lapiths, turning social occasions to blood-baths?" (4: 1.37–40). In fact, Chiron himself has by now become quite civilized: "No weapons of war hung on the walls, no spears and swords that have bathed in human blood. . . . Unlike his boisterous brothers, Chiron had turned his attention to the quiet study of plants' and herbs' medicinal uses" (1.106–10); he is more like one of Statius' high-minded patrons, retired to the country to enjoy the pursuit of wisdom, than the violent teacher of martial arts that myth made of him. Even Chiron's fellow centaurs have grown more sedate, and resent the wild pranks of the young and lawless Achilles (1.146–50).

When Neptune vetoes Thetis' plan to swamp Paris' ship, he explains to the distraught sea-nymph: "That fleet you'd wish to stop in its course is riding a mighty current heaven has set in motion. Europe and Asia will meet in a madness of death and fire. Greek and Trojan blood will turn Ilium's grassy plain to a ghastly bog. What awaits your son is glory, measured in Phrygian gore and tears of widows and orphans who follow the funeral trains of a hero's harvest of corpses" (1.79–86). Statius is not the first poet to put this ironic spin on martial valor, setting the soldier's fame against the context of the grief, the madness, and the wanton bloodshed that are its testimonials. In the previous century, Catullus had included in his poem about the marriage of Peleus and Thetis a hymn sung by the Fates, in which they celebrate the future greatness of the couple's son-to-be, Achilles, in these terms (64.348–51, 362–64, 369–70, 372–73; cf. King 1987: 115–18):

> To his extraordinary virtues and brilliant deeds
> mothers will testify by the deaths of their sons,
> when they loosen the unkempt hair from their white heads
> and bruise their sagging breasts with infirm fists . . .
> and when he's dead, then too a victim will be witness,
> when his rounded tomb piled high into a mound
> receives the snowy limbs of a slain girl . . .
> She, falling like a sacrificial beast to the axe,
> will crumple at the knee and let her slaughtered body sink.
> So come then, join in long-awaited love,
> and let the groom receive the goddess in a blessed bond.

I do not mean to suggest that Statius (or Catullus) was a pacifist, or that he was implicitly criticizing the wars Rome undertook under the direction of the emperor Domitian. The *Achilleid* is not a political manifesto, and Statius would not have dreamed of alienating the ruler whom he was content to address as a god. But this is not to say that his celebration of Achilles constitutes a "justification of Domitian's warlike policy" (Aricò 1986: 2928). Statius understands the phenomenon of war fever, and he is sensitive also to the economic side of military expeditions: note his description of the brisk activity in the copper mines of Cyprus, the cutting of timber for ships in Euboea, the glowing forges where weapons are produced (1.410–34). His epic biography of Achilles betrays the sensibility of a man for whom what mattered in life was literature, cultivated conversation among like-minded people, good dining, and a safe and secure domestic environment. This was not a subversive posture, but it was a civilized one, and that in itself, in most times and places, carries a whiff of dissent.

A notable and touching aspect of the *Achilleid* is Thetis' maternal concern for her son. In the *Iliad*, too, she had lamented the coming death of Achilles, who was doomed, as both knew, to be slain at Troy. When she keens for his destiny along with her sister nymphs, the tone is tragic, but Homer sometimes strikes a more intimate note. Thus, when she dispatched her son to Troy, Thetis thoughtfully packed for him a chest of clean tunics, like a mother carrying a change of underwear to her child in camp (16.220–24). Unlike Homer, however, Statius puts Thetis' anxieties at the center of the action, and the effect is to convert the atmosphere of his poem into something more thoroughly domestic. When Thetis has whisked Achilles off to the island of Scyros, where he awakens lost and confused, like Odysseus just arrived in Ithaca (*Odyssey* 13.187–200; cf. Dante, *Purgatorio* 9.34–39), Thetis tells her son: "If I had married a god, I shouldn't have to worry on your behalf or take these strange precautions." Having thus alluded once again to her frustrated conjugal ambitions, she continues: "But you are mortal, and death lurks everywhere, and I worry—all the time, but these days are worse than any I've seen" (1.250–54).

If Thetis insists here on her fears for Achilles, it is because this is the moment when she must persuade him to put on female attire and conceal himself from the rest of the Greeks in the women's quarters in the palace of Lycomedes, king of Scyros. "'No one,' she reassures him, 'will ever know. It will be our secret, I swear to you'" (1.272–74). Nevertheless, Achilles remains deaf to his mother's appeals, until he sees Deidamia, one of Lycomedes' daughters, in a festive procession. He is instantly smitten. This is a new emotion for him: back in his days with Chiron, it was only to please Thetis that Achilles gave over singing the deeds of heroes in favor of an amatory theme (1.183–85). The representation of the hero in love is another sign that the poet has abandoned the austere conventions of traditional epic for a formula indebted more to romantic elegy, novels, or comic narratives such as the *Metamorphoses* of Ovid. The sober genres, such as epic and tragedy, had tended to avoid the depiction of heroes afflicted by erotic passion. Women might be dominated by such desire—Medea in Apollonius' *Argonautica* is an example, as is Dido in Virgil's *Aeneid*—but in neither case does the hero reciprocate the emotion. There was a story current that Polyxena, a Trojan princess and daughter of Priam, had been betrothed to Achilles; after his death, his ghost returned to demand that she be sacrificed to him in a ghoulish parody of a marriage (the episode, referred to by Catullus, had been dramatized in Euripides' *Hecuba*). For an epic account of Achilles' lovelorn infatuation with Polyxena, however, one must await a prose narrative of the Trojan War, datable probably to a century or so after Statius' time, that purports to be a translation of the eyewitness notes taken by a certain Dictys of Crete (see Merkle 1993; King 1987: 196–201; cf. Latacz, 1995; 21–26).

Thetis at once notices her son's enamorment: "She is thinking aloud how fine it would be to hold in her arms another infant Achilles, a baby her own baby might give her" (1.326–28). Achilles, for his part, immediately agrees to the costume Thetis has proposed, so that he may be near the girl. When Ulysses sees through his disguise, however, the virile Achilles elects to join the expedition to Troy, leaving in her father's care the young princess whom he has raped. The pathos of Deidamia's fears for him, and for herself as well, lest Achilles be tempted by some Trojan maiden, or even by Helen, is reminiscent of the poetic love-letters that Ovid composed (the *Heroides* or "Heroines"), in which various mythological heroines, such as Medea, Ariadne, Penelope, and even Briseis, the war-bride of Achilles, write to the men who have abandoned them. As in Hellenistic lyric and Roman elegy, the grand figures of mythology are humanized in a sentimental vein (cf. Tondoi 1985: 168; Rosati 1994: 9–10). This is the world of sophisticated Roman literature. Whatever Homer's relation to his audience may have been, Statius' *Achilleid* is arm-chair reading, or arm-chair listening, if we imagine the poet declaiming his verses in the palaces of Roman high society he regularly frequented.

Statius could write poetry in a more morbid vein: his *Thebaid*, relating the fratricidal war that brought the kingdom to ruin, its brutal enough for at least one critic to have divined in it an allegory of Rome's own civil strife (Ahl 1986: 2814, 2904). In the *Achilleid*, however, Statius portrayed the hero as boy, and by this indulgent regard for his violent protagonist he struck a tenderly comic note (cf. Fantham 1979: 457, 459; Toohey 1992: 188; contra Aricò 1986: 2959–60), avoiding both the conspiratorial wink of irony and the open derisiveness of burlesque. The posture is simply that of refinement.

Like Statius' *Achilleid*, or what survives of it, Claudian's *The Rape of Proserpine* tells of a goddess' grief for the loss of an adolescent child, who must forsake the games of innocent youth and discover both sexuality and mortality. Of course, there are differences: Ceres—the Latin name for the Greek Demeter, goddess of grain; hence the word "cereal"—laments because her daughter has been carried off by Pluto, king of the underworld, to be his bride, whereas Thetis is delighted at the thought of Achilles' marriage; what distresses her is the prospect of his death while fighting at Troy. For a girl, separation from the mother and incorporation in the household of a husband are analogous to death, and Claudian is sensitive to mortal fear of mother and child alike.

That wedlock for a girl might be conceived not only as a social transaction between male heads of households but also as a rape or violent appropriation is apparent in the earliest of the surviving treatments of the story of Ceres/Demeter and Proserpine/Persephone. The Homeric Hymn to Demeter begins (1–3):

I start up the song of fair-haired Demeter, august goddess—of her and her slim-ankled daughter, whom Hades snatched away, but deep-thundering wide-browed Zeus gave her. (cf. also Hesiod, *Theogony* 912–14)

In the juxtaposition of the words "snatched away" and "gave," the hymn points to a double aspect to Persephone's fate: it is at once an abduction and a proper marriage, in which the father duly bestows his daughter on her husband-to-be. What is more, the two perspectives are those of the mother and father, respectively. This is natural enough, given that Zeus has not had the decency to consult Demeter about his plan to wed the girl to Hades. But Demeter, for her part, seeks to keep her daughter permanently at her side, or at least no further away than the meadow in Sicily where she has been gathering flowers with the Ocean nymphs.

As Homer tells the story, Demeter, in her grief and anger, withdraws from the gods and wanders among the cities of mortals, disguised as an old woman past the age of childbearing. When she arrives in Eleusis—the future site of her famous mysteries—she takes service in the home of a prominent local family as nurse to their first son, Demophoön. The mother, however, interrupts Demeter as she is attempting to render the child immortal by the alarming method of burying him in flames, and in anger the goddess withdraws once again, this time causing a famine upon the earth and an end to sacrificial honors to the gods.

Demeter's decision to descend to earth accords well with her rage against Zeus and Hades, but the story of Demophoön, and Demeter's aborted effort to endow him with immortality, seem something of a digression from the main action (cf. Sfamani Gasparro 1986: 67–77; Clinton 1992: 31–36; Foley 1994: 79, 90, 190–97). Instead of pursuing her search for Persephone, or seeking a way to avenge the loss, Demeter plays nurse and fails in the attempt to elevate a human child to the level of the gods. In addition, when the tale of Demeter's grief for her daughter resumes, Demeter's second withdrawal has the effect of making mortals seem the direct objects and victims of her wrath (see Clay 1989: 205–6).

What is the purpose of the digression, then? Having lost her divine daughter, Demeter descends to earth in order to rear a human child in Persephone's place. By making the infant immortal, she threatens to complete the substitution, displacing her attachment to Persephone onto the now godlike Demophoön. The interruption of the scheme, in turn, has the effect of depriving Demeter for a second time of an immortal child. Like Persephone, Demophoön too must finally descend to Hades. Demeter thus appears to be opposed to change or separation as such. Just as she wishes to keep Persephone forever a girl and prevent her marriage, her attempt to make Demophoön unaging (242, 260) represents another effort to block a change that is natural to human life and to keep a child forever young (Konstan 1996).

And yet, by her threat to destroy both crops and mankind, Demeter ultimately regains the company of Persephone for eight months of the year. Thus she successfully counteracts the pressure toward an alteration of status that is represented by marriage, aging, and death. This is the compromise by which the Homeric Hymn resolves the tension between Zeus' role as proper giver of Persephone and Hades' illegitimate action as abductor: Persephone both is handed over to Hades and remains with her mother, not perpetually, as Demeter might have wished, but in alternation with her sojourns in the underworld. The intersection between Demeter's desire to keep her daughter (from which perspective marriage looks like lawless seizure) and Zeus' authority to give her away in marriage yields the rhythmic equilibrium of the seasonal cycle.

This subtle use of myth to explore the mystery of mortality evolved in the context of agrarian social life and archaic cult practices. The delicate play of symbols would have a hard time retaining its spiritual coherence in the urbane capital of a world empire like that of Rome on the eve of the new millennium. When Ovid takes up the story of Ceres and Proserpine in the fifth book of the *Metamorphoses* (vv. 341–661), he too, like the Homeric Hymn, distributes the narrative into three major sections (for the Hymn's influence here and on the elegiac version in Book 4 of Ovid's *Fasti*, see Hinds 1987). But the resemblance ends here.

Ovid (or rather his persona, the Muse Calliope) begins with the abduction of Proserpine in Sicily (346–437). Calliope then recounts Ceres' search for her daughter, whom she locates thanks to the river-nymph Arethusa, and goes on to relate Ceres' appeal to Jupiter and Jupiter's decision to permit Proserpine to return to her mother's side for six months (not Homer's eight) of the year (438–571). After this—the natural conclusion to the tale of Proserpine's abduction—

Calliope reports that Ceres descended once again to earth to hear Arethusa's story of her own liquefaction as she was fleeing the amorous pursuit of the river god Alpheus (577–641), a narrative almost as long as the description of Proserpine's abduction itself. There follows a brief coda on the fate of Triptolemus (642–61), the inventor of agriculture, with which Calliope concludes her song. Ceres' search for her daughter, as Ovid tells it, is thus reduced to a central panel sandwiched by two narratives of erotic pursuit.

Ovid is a witty and rakish writer, a little like Oscar Wilde but without Wilde's sentimentality, and one expects him to offer a coarser view of the antics of Greek divinities. In his account of the rape of Proserpine, he abolishes the tension between abduction and marriage that was central to the Homeric Hymn, eliminating any reference to Jupiter's role in giving Proserpine to Pluto. Ovid's Pluto is motivated solely by sexual desire. Calliope relates how Venus caught sight of Pluto when he was doing a safety inspection of the area around Mt. Aetna; reminding her son Cupid that he has already conquered Jupiter and Neptune, Venus asks (5.371–72): "Why does Tartarus resist? Why do you not extend your mother's empire and your own? A third of the universe is at stake" (my translation). Venus' reference to her son's empire is Ovid's way of alluding to the ambitions of Augustus, who was alleged to be a descendant of the goddess.

Ovid does everything to emphasize the violence of Pluto's assault and the innocence of Proserpine, who worries childishly about the flowers that drop from the folds of her dress (398–401). When the fountain nymph Cyane attempts to block Pluto's progress, and cries (414–16): "This far and no farther. You cannot do this. This girl is Ceres' daughter, deserving gentler treatment than this. She wants to be wooed and courted" (trans. Slavitt 1994), Pluto drives right by her, and Cyane melts, like Arethusa, into her own waters. Gone is the delicate balance in the Homeric version between the bond with the mother and the transition to marriage; Ovid's is a tale of passionate aggression against a helpless girl.

If Ovid's Pluto is brusquely violent, so too are his goddesses. During Ceres' search for her missing daughter, Ovid relates how she converts a boy who mocks her into a newt. Just because Sicily was the site where her daughter was raped, Ceres, in a fit of rage, turns the once fertile island into a desert. Her punishment of mankind is more deliberate than in the Homeric Hymn, and for that reason more obviously unjust. Even Proserpine gets the opportunity to exact a spiteful vengeance. When a certain Ascaphalus reveals that she has eaten the pomegranate seeds that will oblige her to spend some time each year in the underworld, she transforms him into an owl. All the major actors in the story get to punish some poor character who offends them.

Jupiter is the only figure who shows signs of responsible behavior in the tale, though even his effort at diplomacy comes off as rather sleazy. He tries first to pass off the rape of Proserpine as an act of affection rather than an insult (524–26): "We must put the right names to events and things," he tells Ceres. "Reason demands such precision. Was this a crime, an abduction? Or was it an act of love?" (trans. Slavitt). Caught, however, "between the two irreconcilable gods Pluto and Ceres" (564), Jupiter hits upon the compromise of six months on Olympus for Proserpine, six in Hades. Ceres, who was more indignant at the affront implied by Hades' behavior than distressed by the separation from her daughter as such (513–22), is immediately content with the arrangement. Everyone's pride is salvaged, which is what counts among this bickering aristocratic family, and Ceres can go off happily to hear Arethusa's story about her own misfortune as a young virgin.

Four centuries later, Claudian composed his epic version of the ravishment of Proserpine, which he planned on a far grander scale than any treatment previously known (see the full list of versions in Foley 1994: 30–31). Claudian, though a pagan, was poet laureate at the Christian imperial court in Milan, where he produced verse panegyrics and invectives in the service of his patrons (on his public activity, see Cameron 1970). What meaning could he bring to the ancient tale, long since stripped of awe by the worldly frivolity of Ovid, whose interpretation in the *Metamorphoses*, together with the Homeric Hymn, constitute Claudian's two major sources for his own poem?

Claudian begins his epic in the underworld, where a lonely Pluto vents his rage at his want of wife and children. Thus Claudian brings back into the story the issue of marriage, which Ovid had deleted in favor of a purely erotic motive for the rape. By giving Pluto a personal interest in wedlock, moreover, Claudian has shifted the emphasis away from Ceres' sorrow and Proserpine's terror, which had been central to previous treatments of the myth. Even Pluto, the dread deity of Hell, is now humanized, and for all his Halloween-like bluster he seems almost pathetic in his need for love and family.

Daunted by Pluto's threats that he will return the world to primal chaos if his demand for a wife is not met, the Fates assure him that Jupiter will consent to his marriage. Jupiter ponders the matter, and selects Proserpine as Pluto's bride. Jupiter explains at the beginning of Book III that the wedding will also serve his larger purpose of launching mankind on the path of agriculture and the higher civilized pursuits, since Ceres will impart to humanity the art of sowing and reaping grain as a consequence of the loss and subsequent recovery of her daughter. The world will again enjoy the fertile bounty that had spontaneously flourished in the Golden Age under the rule of Saturn, Jupiter's father, but this time as a result of mortal toil. Proserpine's descent to the underworld, then, is cast as part of a plan that the supreme father on Olympus entertains for the benefit of humanity.

By ascribing a matrimonial motive to Pluto, Claudian renders otiose the role Ovid had assigned to Venus: that of inspiring Pluto with an erotic passion for Proserpine. Claudian is thus free to deploy Venus in another capacity, as Jupiter's agent in luring Proserpine from the fortified castle in Sicily where Ceres had sequestered the girl, so that Pluto may conveniently kidnap her. This move has the consequence of subordinating Venus' function to the mandate of Jupiter. On a symbolic level, moreover, the fact that Venus has a hand in enticing Proserpine from her sanctuary suggests that she may, despite her youth, have been ready to abandon the seclusion to which her mother's protectiveness had consigned her and to accept wedlock. Indeed, as Claudian tells it, Proserpine was already the object of suitors' attentions while she was still on Olympus; it was to shield her from the rival claims of Mars and Apollo that Ceres whisked her off to Sicily in the first place.

Later, as Pluto bears Proserpine away in his chariot, he assuages her fears with a vision of life in the underworld that makes of it a paradise. In a pastiche derived from Orphic and other sources, largely by way of Virgil's image of Hades in the *Aeneid* (Book 6), Pluto explains: "We too have stars, and meadows, and flowers that never fade" (2.282–83)—the Latin here specifies another sun as well. In his joyous mood, Pluto more than makes good on his promises, as all Hell breaks out in festive celebration: insubstantial spirits sit down to dinner, the torments of sinners are suspended, and death itself takes a holiday. Proserpine has her wedding party, in Claudian's version, before her mother is even aware that she is missing.

This Elysian image of the underworld is, as scholars have noticed, a far cry from the gloomy picture Claudian evokes at the beginning of his poem, when Pluto first bewails his bachelorhood (cf. Gruzelier 1993: xxvi–xxvii, 92). It is true that Claudian, like the poets of his age generally, relishes cameo scenes, and tends to juxtapose brilliant descriptive passages like gems in an elaborate ornament—what Michael Roberts (1989) has called "the jeweled style" in late antique literature—without taking equal care to integrate them into a logically coherent narrative of the sort one expects from a modern novel. David Slavitt recognizes Claudian's predilection for the stunning set piece with the witty formula, "first slide, please" (1.149), which exactly captures the sense of a sequence of select scenes. More to the point, however, is that the emotional trajectory of the poem in the first two books proceeds from the bleakness of Pluto's lonely reign in Hell to the cosmic and universal joy that accompanies his marriage. At the beginning of the final book of the poem as Claudian left it, Jupiter will ratify the marriage as the basis for a new epoch in which human beings will give over their primitive diet of acorns and learn the art of farming and, with that, attain to modern civilization. It is easy to imagine that Hell too might have altered in the process.

Claudian's Jupiter is an autocratic monarch, and he controls his council with the firm command of a late Roman emperor. Claudian, as court poet, knew the manner well. Virginal goddesses like Diana and Minerva may grumble at the way they were unwittingly exploited to allay the suspicions of Proserpine and favor Venus' plan (indeed, Proserpine's servant Electra supposes that they were actively in on the plot), but they are in no position to object to Jupiter's design, and will loyally keep silent about Proserpine's whereabouts when Ceres storms up to Olympus to deliver her frenzied complaints. Rebuffed, Ceres sets off to cut herself a gigantic pair of torches in a copse in the vicinity of Mt. Aetna, with which to light her way as she pursues the tracks of her daughter. "This grove is sacred: not even the Cyclops ventures there, but Ceres is undeterred. The sanctity only serves to provoke her" (3.340–42). The learned reader may recall that when the Hellenistic poet Callimachus (third-century B.C.) composed his Hymn to Demeter, he substituted for the story of Persephone a quite different episode, in which Demeter punishes the prince Erysichthon for impiously cutting down trees in a hallowed grove. Claudian's frantic Ceres is at the opposite pole from Callimachus' composed and fair-minded goddess. The scene makes for good thrills, but it also duplicates Virgil's theology in the *Aeneid*, in which the grand scheme for human history ratified by the father of gods and men is accomplished by way of Juno's passionate violence and Venus' seductive wiles (see Konstan 1986).

Claudian's poem breaks off as Ceres commences her search, her gloomy brands, fashioned of cypresses, reminding her of the torches she had hoped one day to carry at her daughter's wedding (3.405–8). The connection between connubial and funereal ceremonies is a commonplace in classical literature (Rehm 1994), but it has special point in Claudian's epic inasmuch as Proserpine is at this very moment celebrating her wedding to the god of the underworld. Ceres' hopes for her daughter's marriage introduce a sentimental note that may seem at odds with her earlier effort to hide the child from suitors, but Claudian's conception of the rape of Proserpine has from the beginning also had the quality of a sacred union or *hieros gamos*, in which a divine marriage is figured as a sign of cosmic renewal. Ceres is not simply a possessive mother, such as she appears in the Homeric Hymn, who wishes to keep her baby forever at her side. While it is not to be expected that she would voluntarily have chosen Pluto for her son-in-law, one may suppose that she would ultimately have reconciled herself to Proserpine's residence in Hell, especially given its cheery new look since the abduction.

Composing new variations on old mythic themes, and elaborating the set graphic pieces that the ancients called ecphrases—a learned disquisition on volcanoes, a catalogue of flowers in a meadow, or the detailed description of images on a tapestry like the one Proserpine was weaving in her Sicilian citadel when Venus and the other goddesses came to visit her—make for good entertainment; such bits evidently appealed to audiences in Claudian's time, and they can still do so today, when one reads them in a sensitive and witty adaptation like that of David Slavitt. Beyond such rhetorical figures, Claudian has a refined feel for human psychology, and makes the ancient deities come alive as characters, not just as abstract forces of nature.

But one may nevertheless wonder why a sophisticated poet of panegyrics in a Christian imperial court should have chosen to narrate once again an old pagan myth about Jupiter's decision to bestow his daughter in wedlock upon the lord of the underworld, where, despite her initial terror and her mother's protectiveness, she will contribute to bringing about a new era in the history of mankind and harmony between the supernal and nether divinities. At a time when the celebration of pagan mysteries of the sort associated with Ceres and Proserpine was repressed by the Christian state, even an ostensibly literary evocation of the old myth in an elevated genre such as epic may have registered as a gesture of protest. Was this scintillating recreation of a divine child's descent to the world below at her father's far-seeing command, her suffering and her ultimate resurrection and triumph as judge and queen of the dead, designed to demonstrate that Greek myth, suitably modernized according to the taste of the age, could still evoke the sense of sacrifice and transcendence that the Christian narrative conveyed? It is impossible to know—the explicit references to Christianity in the translation, the reader should be aware, are Slavitt's rather than Claudian's, though to me they seem to strike the right note of humane rivalry between the old beliefs and the new. It may be that Claudian, like his contemporary Symmachus (*Relatio* 3), considered that there were many paths by which one might arrive at the common mystery, and that his epic poem about the goddesses, mother and daughter, whose rites were among the most revered in pagan antiquity, intimated to those who sympathized a vision parallel to the sacred story of Christianity.

References

Ahl, Frederick M. 1986. "Statius' 'Thebaid': A Reconsideration." *Aufstieg und Niedergang der Romischen Welt* II.32.5 (ed. H. Temporini and W. Haase): 2803–2912.

Aricò, Giuseppi. 1986. "L' 'Achilleide' di Stazio: tradizione letteraria e invenzione narrativa." *Aufstieg und Niedergang der Romischen Welt* II.32.5 (ed. H. Temporini and W. Haase): 2925–64.

Ballabriga, Alain. 1996. "Le Cent-Bras Briarée, fils de Zeus plus fort que son père: Une correction de la *Théogonie* (886–900) dans l'*Iliade* (I, 393–406)." *Kernos* 9: 257–70.

Cameron, Alan. 1970. *Claudian: Poetry and Propaganda at the Court of Honorius.* Oxford: Oxford University Press.

Clay, Jenny Strauss. 1989. *The Politics of Olympus: Form and Meaning in the Major Homeric Hymns.* Princeton, N.J.: Princeton University Press.

Clinton, Kevin. 1992. *Myth and Cult: The Iconography of the Eleusinian Mysteries.* Stockholm: Acta Instituti Atheniensis Regni Sueciae.

Dilke, O. A. W., ed. 1954. *Statius: Achilleid.* Cambridge: Cambridge University Press. Reprint New York: Arno Press, 1979.

Fantham, Elaine. 1979. "Statius' Achilles and His Trojan Model." *Classical Quarterly* n.s. 29: 457–62.

Foley, Helene P., ed. 1994. *The Homeric Hymn to Demeter.* Princeton, N.J.: Princeton University Press, 1994.

Gruzelier, Claire, ed. 1993. *Claudian: De raptu Proserpinae.* Oxford: Clarendon Press.

Haasse, Hella S. 1993. *Threshold of Fire: A Novel of Fifth Century Rome*, trans. Anita Miller and Nini Blinstrub. Chicago: Academy Chicago.

King, Katherine Callen. 1987. *Achilles: Paradigms of the War Hero from Homer to the Middle Ages.* Berkeley: University of California Press.

Hinds, Stephen. 1987. *The Metamorphoses of Persephone: Ovid and the Self-Conscious Muse.* Cambridge: Cambridge University Press.

Konstan, David. 1986. "Venus's Enigmatic Smile." *Vergilius* 32: 18–25.

Konstan, David. 1996. "De Deméter a Ceres: Construcciones de la diosa en Homero, Calímaco y Ovidio." *Synthesis* 3: 67–90.

Kossatz-Deissmann, Anneliese. 1981. "Achilles." *LIMC* I: 55–69.

Latacz, Joachim. 1995. *Achilleus: Wandlungen eines europäischen Heldenbildes.* Stuttgart and Leipzig: Teubner.

Merkle, Stefan. 1994. "Telling the True Story of the Trojan War: The Eyewitness Account of Dictys of Crete." In James Tatum, ed., *The Search for the Ancient Novel* (Baltimore: Johns Hopkins University Press).

Mozley, J. H. 1928. *Statius*, vol. 2. Cambridge, Mass.: Harvard University Press; London: W. Heinemann.

Radt, Stefan, ed. 1977. *Tragicorum Graecorum fragmenta.* Vol. 4: *Sophocles.* Göttingen: Vandehoek and Ruprecht.

Rehm, Rush. 1994. *Marriage to Death: The Conflation of Wedding and Funeral Rituals in Greek Tragedy.* Princeton, N.J.: Princeton University Press.

Roberts, Michael. 1989. *The Jeweled Style: Poetry and Poetics in Late Antiquity.* Ithaca, N.Y.: Cornell University Press.

Rosati, Gianpiero, ed. 1994. *Stazio: Achilleide.* Milan: Rizzoli.

Roussel, Monique. 1991. *Biographie légendaire d'Achille.* Amsterdam: A. M. Hakkert.

Sfamani Gasparro, Giulia. 1986. *Misteri e culti: mistici di Demetra.* Rome: Bretschneider.

Slavitt, David R. 1994. "Pagans and Poets." *Newsday,* Jan. 2.

Slavitt, David R., trans. 1994. *The Metamorphoses of Ovid.* Baltimore: Johns Hopkins University Press.

Tondoi, Vincenzo. 1985. "Gli epici di fine I secolo dopo Cristo, o il crepuscolo degli dei." *Atene e Roma* 30: 154–69.

Toohey, Peter. 1992. *Reading Epic: An Introduction to the Ancient Narratives.* London: Routledge.

Turner, Victor. 1969. *The Ritual Process: Structure and Anti-Structure.* Chicago: Aldine. Reprint New York: Aldine de Gruyter, 1995.